THE PARTY BOOK

THE PARTY BOOK

Kathie Webber

Elm Tree Books
Hamish Hamilton · London

First published in Great Britain 1975
by Elm Tree Books Ltd
90 Great Russell Street, London WC1

SBN 241 89199 X

Photographs by Mike Leale
China by courtesy of Wedgwood and available from
Gered, 158 Regent Street, London W1
Cutlery and silverware from WMF (Britain) Ltd
All paperware products manufactured by Deeko Ltd
Drawings by Stuart Honey

Cover shows a centrepiece of frosted fruit

This book has been produced by Elm Tree Books,
Hamish Hamilton Ltd, in collaboration with
Deeko Ltd, manufacturers of paper tableware

Printed in Great Britain by
Ebenezer Baylis and Son Limited
The Trinity Press
Worcester and London

Contents

Introduction

GATHERING TOGETHER THE recipes for this book and thinking about the kinds of parties one can give has generated an enormous excitement in me to go straight into the actual practice of entertaining after considering the theory. For each situation I've thought about, lists of real guests, specific menus and ideas for table-settings have sprung to mind, and, happily, these plans are now turning into actual party-giving dates. There are so many ways of entertaining: from enjoying a quiet dinner with two close friends to inviting forty people round for drinks in the garden in summer; from getting the family together for a silver wedding buffet, to having all the kids round to celebrate a child's birthday. There is no single formula for a wonderful get-together.

The secret of entertaining lies in what I've been doing these last few weeks ... planning. Plan any party well enough and the actual doing is enormous fun for the host and hostess as well as for the guests. Sadly, too many people embark on an evening with little forethought and spend the whole time worrying that the food won't be eaten or that there won't be enough to drink or people will spill things or that guests won't get on together. The list of possible ways in which you can ruin a party for yourself is endless.

I believe that one's duty to one's friends ends after the invitations have been sent, food and drink has been provided in quantities sufficient to ensure that no one goes away hungry or thirsty, and every effort has been made to give everyone a great time. The fact that your sister has argued for hours with your best friend could indicate it's been the most stimulating evening either has had for a long time, though perhaps not the most comfortable for you as the hostess. All the planning in the world cannot determine how people will react to each other, though you can be certain they'll enjoy themselves.

Naturally, the amount of trouble you take to make your party a success plays a huge part in your reputation as a hostess. Although many aspects of party-giving simply aren't vital, it adds to everyone's enjoyment if the hostess has a few skills up her sleeve. Skills such as flower-arranging, napkin-folding, artistic ways with table linen and crockery colours, and bright ideas with candles, centrepieces, themes for parties, gifts and so on—all of these can make a gathering of friends very special, whether it's a budget supper for four or a grand 'do' for dozens.

Whatever the number of guests, the season, the place or the menu, there are several basic rules which apply to each and every party, and these are all summarised in this introduction.

Deciding at what point to limit the numbers of your guests is always difficult. It's no problem if you're giving a dinner party because you invite the number of people your table will seat comfortably—four, six or eight, usually. Buffets, too, are easy. You'll have a fair idea already of how many people you can accommodate in your home, but it's worth remembering that as the evening progresses people may sit on the floor, so don't invite the maximum number of people the room will hold on the assumption that they will all stand all of the time. Another tip to note is that people don't circulate freely. Provide them with two rooms and you'll find everyone crammed into one or the other room at any one time unless, of course, you've invited enough guests to make sure they naturally overspill into the hall, kitchen, dining room or wherever.

Garden parties are a wonderful way of entertaining lots of people and if good weather could be guaranteed, numbers would be of no concern. But sadly, it's wise to limit the numbers to the amount you can accommodate inside should the weather be unsuitable or change during the course of the party. (This also applies to barbecues and bonfire-night parties.)

Children's parties should be kept small—six or eight kids are enough, whatever their ages. It's impossible to keep an eye on more and the noise and destruction will increase twofold for every extra guest. Family parties also pose their problems. One feels obliged to ask everyone even when the house won't cope. In such a situation, there would seem to be a case for altering the type of party rather than upsetting one's relations. Plan a buffet party rather than a dinner party. A very special tea party can be given instead of a drinks party if the numbers have grown too many for your budget.

I get very annoyed with people who have a number fixation where parties are concerned. It doesn't matter that the numbers are odd or that one or more guests don't have partners. When you invite someone to a party, remember it's for a few hours, not for life, so it isn't necessary to settle them with a mate at 7 o'clock in the evening. It may make your guests feel uncomfortable if you make it clear they must come with a partner to keep your numbers even, or, alternatively, come on their own to make a regular total. Recently, I received an invitation to a dinner party which was cancelled on the morning of the party itself because I'd accepted gladly but said I'd be on my own that evening. They found it better to upset me by cancelling at the last moment than to have a 'spare' female. That's the worst crime in entertaining; don't ever be guilty of it.

Invitations are very informal nowadays. Using the phone is quite acceptable for family, friends and children, and it's certainly easier to use the phone to invite large numbers for a buffet. But if you want to set a slightly more formal tone, a brief hand-written note will suffice. The typewriter used to be taboo for invitations —but not any more, though it's considered more polite and friendly to write by hand. Printed cards are fun, and there are many varieties for children's parties. On them you write the occasion, address, date and any other details. Children love to receive letters, so it's worth spending a few extra pence on some colourful cards (which your children should write and send, not you). Formal invitations have fallen completely out of use except perhaps for such occasions as wedding breakfasts or engagement parties.

Allow ample time for menu planning, taking into consideration the season, the number of guests, individual likes and dislikes (if known), how much work you'll want to do beforehand, and the amount of money available. It's a good idea to get the starters and puddings done the day before for dinner parties; sandwiches, cakes and buns for tea parties; and pâtés and quiches for buffets. If you have a freezer then almost all of every menu can be prepared and tucked away, to be removed on the day to thaw—and perhaps later to be decorated or garnished, or cooked and finished. It's worth planning your menu around dishes with which you are familiar. Don't try out something new unless you're an accomplished cook or have something else to offer should you find you have a failure on your hands.

Table-settings can be subtly altered for each occasion even though, like most people, you may be limited to one dinner service, best tablecloth and cutlery. Descriptions of people bringing out their Mexican dinner service to complement the glass they bought in Venice and using the little silk scarves picked up for £5 in Outer Mongolia for napkins irritate me immensely, especially as I rely for my colour and interest on soft paper napkins—those cushiony, colourful squares that tempt one to buy dozens of different packets at once. Even with one cloth and one dinner service, there are usually one or two colours you can pick out with paper napkins to give different kinds of table settings. It's possible to change the setting by using a flower arrangement one time, candles another and frosted fruit a third. Using large mats instead of a cloth can give yet another look to your table. Try to vary the setting as much as possible, complementing food with the table's appearance each time. I have a friend who makes napkins from oddments of cloth found in sales, and these turn her dinner table into something out of a bistro, an Italian restaurant, granny's dining room or whatever takes her fancy when she's planning.

Seating arrangements must be planned when catering for dozens of people but it's seldom necessary for a small dinner party, except perhaps to separate a husband and wife or ensure that all the men or women aren't together. But round a small table it really isn't vital to decide in advance who will sit where.

One of the major problems of a party can be where to put coats, particularly when it's raining. Brollies go straight in the bath—no trouble—and it's worth putting up a temporary coat rail over the bath. A broom handle on the windowsill, the other end on the steps of a step-ladder will do. The alternative is to dump coats on a bed, which isn't a good idea because your guest will have to get into damp, creased clothes at the end of a super evening.

For a few pence, candles set an atmosphere quicker than anything else I know. Besides being very flattering for ladies, they're also immensely flattering to a room that could do with a lick of paint. Candles are the cheapest and easiest way of lighting the garden, for garden parties and for barbecues, but will blow out unless protected. If you have a bottle-cutting kit or know someone who has one, you can cut lots of bottles down to cylinders and use these glass shades to protect the candle flame from the wind. Push the candles into the earth in flower borders and stick the shade into the earth to surround the candle.

Indoors, two or three candles in the centre of the dining table will provide all the light you need. You can arrange them to form a centrepiece by pushing them into plasticine and then sticking flower heads and leaves in the plasticine to cover it. Don't bypass bunches of parsley or mint when you're searching for something with which to decorate the table. Lemon verbena, thyme and other herbs look very pretty and will also give off an attractive scent if you bruise the leaves gently. Dried leaves and flowers can take the place of the fresh varieties in winter and fruit and nuts can be used effectively too.

Spectacular centrepieces can be made by frosting fruit. It is a little bit extravagant, but if you're after an original effect, this is how you do it. Lightly whisk some egg white, dip in the fruit and brush it well. Sprinkle with caster sugar to coat it completely and leave to dry. Frosting works well with apples and plums or bunches of grapes, whole ones or small clusters. When the fruit is quite dry, arrange it on a glass cakestand or on a plate standing on a stemmed glass to raise it from the table. Secure it with plasticine. Grape clusters can hang over the edge and you can add to the centrepiece according to the occasion: raspberry leaves for a summer garden party or mint sprigs, dried flowers and grasses for autumn buffets, baubles and tinsel for parties around Christmas, ribbons for wedding breakfasts, engagements and so on. Special centrepieces and table decorations which can be bought in shops are described in the chapters on toddlers', children's and celebration parties.

Doilies come and go in fashion. Currently they're in favour, very pretty and essential for tea parties, to set off arrangements of sandwiches and cakes. White ones are most usual, but the gold and silver doilies can be used most effectively for silver wedding parties, weddings, Christmas, birthday buffets and so on. Have a look at the photograph on the front cover. It shows the frosted fruits centrepiece described above but I've added gold and silver doilies, bunched and tucked here and there between the fruits to add some sparkle.

Children love to help put their own parties together. Even the little ones can help by making their own doilies, or colouring plain (bought) ones, or cutting their own sandwiches into shapes with animal cutters. It doesn't matter if they're not perfect—lack of perfection isn't something that bothers us until we grow older. Napkin-folding is an art I've often wanted to master: not the complicated shapes that restaurants use which aren't always suitable for the home anyway, but just something that's a bit different and will enhance my table setting. The picture strips on the following pages instruct in the art of folding some of the prettier shapes. Like many of the little party pieces, it isn't necessary but it all helps to make one's reputation as a hostess.

Unless it's a buffet rather than a straightforward dinner party, catering equipment can be a headache. Borrow rather than hire if you can, to save expense. But remember you'll need $1\frac{1}{2}$ times everything for a large buffet because people have a habit of not remembering where they left their glasses, plates and cutlery. Two of everything is better if you're giving the party in the garden and particularly if it's

Buffet

This can be made with a single napkin or 2 same-size napkins in different colours. Instructions are for 2 napkins. To start, open napkins and lay one on top of the other. 1. Fold napkins twice into a ¼-sized square, open edges on top and right side. Fold down upper right corner in 2 thicknesses with points at the exact middle of the square. 2. Fold down again twice so that the napkin is cut by a diagonal as in 3. 4. Fold 1 more edge and tuck into pocket at the middle. 5. Fold the 2 sides under to meet at the back. 6. Tuck cutlery inside pocket.

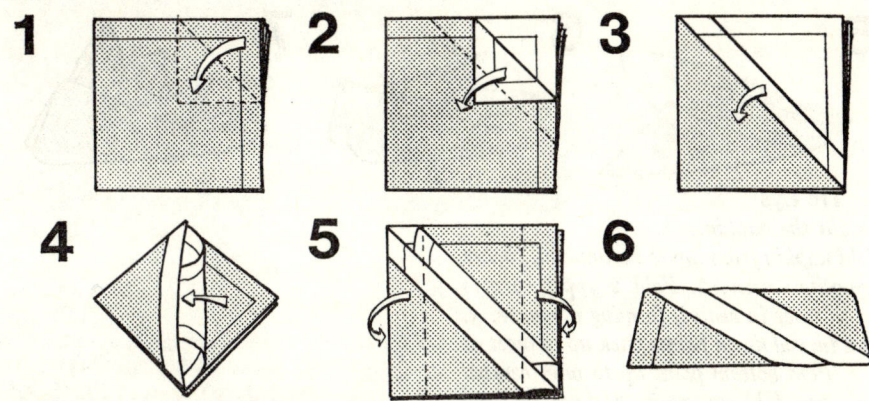

Princess

Open out the napkin. 1. Make 2 accordion pleats, from the top and the bottom to meet exactly in the middle of the napkin. 2. Fold back each pleat along the exact middle to give 3 open edges on top. 3. Accordion pleat once from both sides to meet in centre. 4. Fold top flap into triangle and press hard. 5 & 6. Make triangles with each flap, reversing crease in middle of each pleat. 7. Arrange.

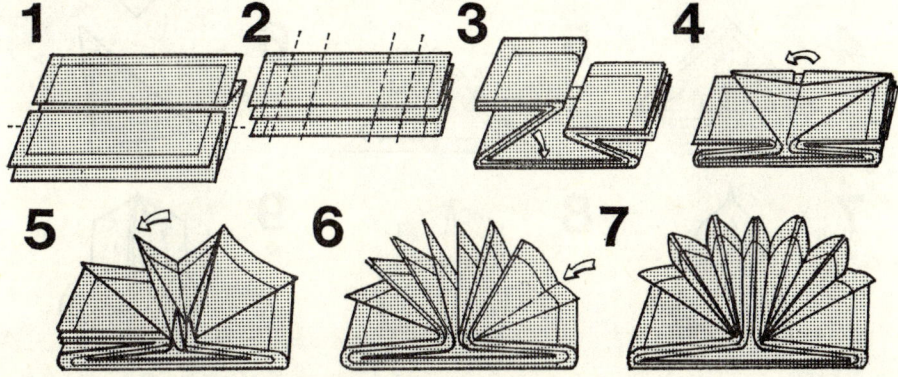

Cockscomb

1. Fold napkin into 4 and then again across diagonally with open edges up. 2. Fold in sides to meet at the middle. 3. Fold bottom points back under and press flat. 4. Fold back napkin on middle crease to look like 5. 6. Pull out loose points so that the napkins looks like 7.

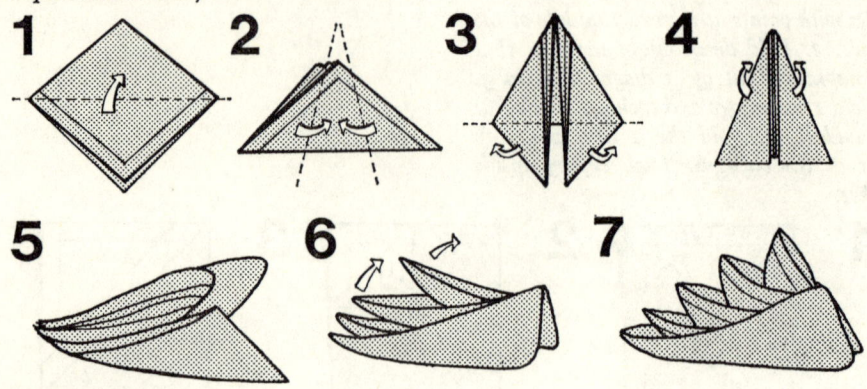

Fleur De Lys

Open out the napkin.

1. Fold napkin from top to bottom and corner to opposite corner. 2. Fold 2 upper corners down to meet in centre, forming a square. 3. Fold 2 turned down points back up to meet at top. 4. Fold bottom point up to meet central edges, then fold up again 3 times to form collar overlapping the upper part. 5. Bend napkin and insert one point of the collar into the other to secure as in 6 & 7. 8. Turn down the 2 loose flaps and tuck them into collar to give 9.

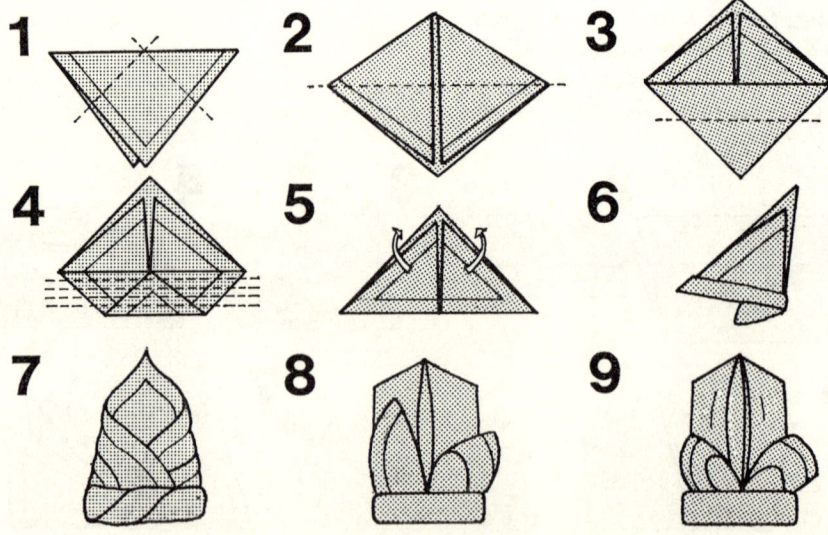

to be at night. Glasses get lost in the grass and aren't easy to find again in the dark. Paper plates, cups and napkins are ideal for this kind of party because they can simply be stuffed into a huge sack and left by the bin, saving time and tempers later. If you have to hire, go for the firm that takes away the stuff dirty—you have to stack it back into its boxes but the washing up is all part of the price per ten items (metric nowadays). These companies will provide items such as huge cloths, trestle tables, chairs, ham stands, wedding-cake stands, carving equipment, cake knives and silver coffee sets as well as the usual plates, cutlery and glasses. Ask for a brochure when you ring for quotations.

Taking a gift to one's hostess is a nice thought. Wine is sometimes offered but a cheaper and perfectly acceptable alternative might be a box of after-dinner mints. But it's worth going to a bit more trouble and buying half a pound of hand-made chocolates rather than the ready-packed mints. If you know your hostess has a particular weakness for chocolate ginger or fudge, then take her a quarter pound, but make it something just for her to show you appreciate the trouble she's going to on your behalf.

It is sad that so few people bother nowadays with thank-you notes. When someone sends *me* a note saying how much they enjoyed the evening it gives me another chance to enjoy my glory all over again. One lovely man I know always used to send me a single flower after a dinner party with a note saying 'Great evening, thank you' —or similar words. However, even this forethought (as it turned out) went astray one day when I realised he organised the flower before he'd even been for dinner. After a particularly ferocious evening when one guest attacked another on politics, my friend ended up by walking out in a fury. I was astonished to receive the usual flower with the same note. So it's not worth thinking that far in advance if you intend sending a thank-you note.

1

Buffet Parties

EASILY THE MOST popular form of party-giving is the buffet, which enables you to entertain lots of people without having to provide the right amount of chairs and table space to seat everyone. Another important reason, for me the best one, is that a buffet meal can be prepared well in advance so it should be one of the least exhausting kinds of party. Even if you don't actually manage to put your feet up for half an hour beforehand, at least during the party you can be as relaxed as your guests.

Buffets don't differ much whatever the season but the seasons do allow lots of lovely opportunities for decorating your table differently or for having your party outside on the terrace or lawn during the summer months. There is a whole set of rules which applies only to the buffet party.

1. People won't stand all the time so put cushions on the floor to encourage a relaxed atmosphere.
2. Once people are relaxed they tend to put their glasses and plates anywhere they can find a horizontal surface. Don't provide your best cut glass, and remove the most precious books, ornaments and potted plants to a room which won't be used.
3. Beg, borrow or hire plates, glasses and cutlery. For each item, you'll need $1\frac{1}{2}$ times the number of people you've invited. It's possible (though awkward) to wash odd things during a dinner party but out of the question at a buffet. Make sure you have enough of the basic items.
4. Allow plenty of paper napkins. Paper ones are the best because they'll quickly absorb any spills.
5. A buffet relies largely on the display of your food, which means giving much thought to the table covering. A large plain white cloth could make a dull background unless relieved by colour. Again, use paper napkins, or alternatively, the colourful paper table covers which are now available to match almost any decor. Should you want to set the food on different levels (which is a useful trick if your table is large), stand wooden boxes on your table at the back and cover them with your cloth: thus giving you two levels. Savouries can go in front, and at the back on the higher level display your sweets, flowers and other delicacies.

6. Prepare your menu, bearing in mind that a lot of things should be done the day before. Allow, if possible, the morning of the party for arranging the table and adding decorations and garnishes to the dishes you're preparing. Obviously if you're preparing hot foods you will have to do some work on the day but this can be trimmed to a minimum with planning.

7. Prepare food in bite-sized pieces or at least make sure it can be tackled with a fork alone. I've found the only way to cope with a buffet meal is to grab a large plate, put on a little food (little is important, because there must be space left to stand your glass). A napkin can be held between the fingers of the left hand and the plate can stand on your open palm. Left-handers reverse these instructions. You can eat well, you have a free hand and you aren't desperately bobbing up and down juggling with crockery.

8. Don't worry if the cutlery seems to be disappearing unevenly. People seem to be perfectly happy using a spoon for cheese and a knife and their fingers for the main course, should the right implements not be available.

9. If the buffet is very large and you are making more than one of the same dish, then it's worth splitting the food items on the table. It gives guests two chances to reach the same food and will prevent those long queues which are the quickest conversation-killer I know. Quantities can be difficult but here is a guide to amounts. *Fork buffet*: allow per person, 1 starter, 1 main savoury dish, 1 sweet and 3–4 drinks. If you want to provide alternatives, remember guests will always have something of everything so if you do half-quantities only you'll find half your guests going without a pudding or whatever.

Finger buffet: allow per person 4–6 savoury items, 2 sweet items such as éclairs or meringues or trifle and 3–4 drinks.

General quantities:

salted nuts	$\frac{1}{2}$ ounce per person
potato crisps	1 ounce per person
cocktail snacks	5–6 per person
1 sandwich loaf (large)	20 slices
6 ounces creamed butter	spreads 1 large sandwich loaf
1 long French loaf	cuts into 20 1-inch slices

Sandwich fillings:

1 pound thinly-sliced cooked meat	fills 16 rounds
12 chopped hard-boiled eggs	fills 16 rounds
1 pound grated cheese mixed with creamed butter and chopped chives	fills 16 rounds
8-ounce tin salmon mixed with mayonnaise	fills 4 rounds

Pastry items:

1 pound shortcrust pastry makes	48 pastry cases (use $2\frac{1}{2}$-inch cutter)
	24 mince pies
	4 7-inch flan cases
	3 8-inch flan cases
	2 7-inch double crust pies

Meat, poultry and fish:

cooked joint of meat with bone	6–8 ounces per person
cooked joint of meat without bone	4–6 ounces per person
steak	6–8 ounces per person
sliced cold meats	4 ounces per person
chicken	8 ounces per person or 1 chicken joint
white fish	6 ounces per person
salmon	6 ounces per person
scampi	6–8 ounces per person

Other main-course items:

savoury sauces	$\frac{1}{2}$ pint for 4 people
mayonnaise	1 pint for 12 people
soups	$\frac{1}{4}$–$\frac{1}{3}$ pint per person
potatoes	$\frac{1}{2}$ pound unpeeled per person
peas	4–6 ounces per person
rice	$1\frac{1}{2}$–2 ounces uncooked per person
spaghetti	3 ounces uncooked per person

Sweets and desserts:

strawberries	6 ounces per person
raspberries	4 ounces per person
double cream	1 pint for 10 people
fruit salad	2 pints for 6–8 people
fruit mousse	2 pints for 6–8 people
custard	1 pint for 4–6 people
Victoria sandwich	7-inch for 6 people

gâteau	9-inch for 8 people
meringues using 6 egg whites, 12 ounces sugar and ¾ pint cream	48 meringues or 24 sandwiched together
ice cream	2 family-size blocks for 12 people or ½ gallon for 20 people
trifle made with 4 pints custard, 25 trifle sponge cakes and 1 large tin of fruit	enough for 25 people

Drinks:

wine	6–8 glasses per bottle
champagne	6–8 glasses per bottle
fruit squash	20 glasses per bottle
gin/whisky	20 single measures per bottle
sherry	12 glasses per bottle
port	10–12 glasses per bottle
liqueurs	32 small glasses per bottle

Punch is often the least expensive way of providing a beverage. People always drink punch like lemonade so while it's worth making the first batch strong enough for people to notice, I've found it better to make successive bowls less strong and more fruity.

Cheese Aigrettes

2 ounces plain flour (sifted)
good pinch salt
1 ounce butter
¼ pint cold water
1 large egg
2 ounces Cheddar cheese (grated)
oil or fat for deep frying
1 ounce Parmesan cheese (grated)

PUT THE FLOUR to warm. Put the salt, butter and cold water in a pan. Bring to the boil. Remove from the heat and add the flour all at once. Beat well until the mixture is smooth and leaves the sides of the pan clean. When the pan is cool enough to stand on the palm of your hand, beat in the egg well, then beat in the Cheddar cheese.

Form the mixture into small balls and fry until golden brown. Drain well on absorbent kitchen paper and serve sprinkled with Parmesan cheese.

Serves 6

Apple Punch (non-alcoholic)

½ pint cold water
2-inch cinnamon stick
pinch ground nutmeg
2 whole cloves
2 ounces granulated sugar
2 pints apple juice
½ pint fresh orange juice
juice of 1 lemon (strained)
mint sprigs

POUR THE WATER into a pan. Add the spices and sugar and heat to dissolve the sugar. Then bring to the boil and simmer for about 15 minutes until syrupy. Pour the apple and orange juices into a serving bowl. Add the lemon juice and strain on the spiced syrup. Stir well and serve well chilled, decorated with mint sprigs.
Serves 6

Mulled Wine

1 bottle dry white wine
1 bottle rosé
3 ounces granulated sugar
3 whole cardamom seeds
1 blade mace
2-inch cinnamon stick
1 bay leaf
rind of 1 orange (thinly pared)
2 ounces stoned raisins
white grapes
1 small egg white (beaten)
caster sugar

POUR THE WINES into a pan. Add the sugar and the spices and bay leaf tied in a muslin bag. Add the orange rind and raisins. Bring slowly to the boil, remove from heat and cover.

Divide the grapes into 3-sprig bunches. Dip in egg white and caster sugar, shaking off excess. Allow to dry. Stir the raspberry conserve into the punch, remove the spice bag and orange rind and serve in heatproof glasses, each decorated with frosted grapes.
Serves 8

3 level tablespoons raspberry conserve

Strawberry Fizz

4 tablespoons brandy
4 ounces strawberries
1 bottle red wine (chilled)
2 pints fizzy lemonade
white grapes

POUR THE BRANDY over the strawberries and leave for 30 minutes. Put them in a punch bowl, pour on the wine and the lemonade just before serving. Add sprigs of white grapes.
Serves 10

Spiced Fruit Punch (non-alcoholic)

28-ounce can apricot halves
½ pint cold water
2 2-inch cinnamon sticks
½ level teaspoon whole allspice
6 whole cloves
1 level teaspoon ground
  ginger
2 blades mace
juice of 1 lemon (strained)
19-ounce can pineapple juice
½ pint orange juice

DRAIN THE APRICOTS and pour ½ pint juice into a large pan. Add the water and spices and simmer for 10 minutes. Pour the lemon juice and other fruit juices into another pan. Sieve or blend the apricot halves and the remaining juice and add to the pan. Bring to boiling point. Strain the spiced syrup into the fruit juices, stir well. Pour into a large bowl and serve in punch glasses.
Serves 8

½ pint grapefruit juice

Sauce Verte

Mayonnaise:

1 large egg yolk
pinch mustard powder
pinch salt
pinch caster sugar
pinch pepper
¼ pint salad oil
1 tablespoon wine vinegar or
  white vinegar
2 teaspoons lemon juice
  (strained)

Colouring and flavouring:

watercress
parsley
tarragon (optional)
  (preferably fresh)

PUT THE YOLK into a small bowl. Add the seasonings and sugar and using a small whisk or wooden spoon, beat the egg yolk well. Begin to add the oil, a drop at a time, beating well after each addition. Too much oil added at this stage could curdle the mixture. If it looks like it might curdle, stop adding oil and beat like mad. Continue adding oil a little more quickly after you have used just over half the amount. Stir in the vinegar and lemon juice.

Should your mayonnaise curdle, break another yolk into a clean bowl and add the curdled mayonnaise slowly, beating all the time.

Roughly chop about 2 level teaspoons of watercress (amount after chopping not before) and the same each of parsley and tarragon. Put the herbs and mayonnaise in a blender and blend for 30 seconds. Taste for seasoning and blend again for 30 seconds if not quite mixed. The colour should be a pale green, so adjust the amount of herbs added if the sauce is too light.

Serves 8

Quick White Rolls

1-pound packet white soda
  bread mix
2 ounces margarine
11 ounces water
plain flour

EMPTY THE CONTENTS of the packet into a bowl. Rub in the margarine and make a well in the centre. Add all the water and mix to a soft dough. Sprinkle with a little flour, knead lightly and form into 15 rolls. Arrange on greased baking sheets and bake for about 25 minutes or until golden brown at Gas 7/425°F.

Makes 15

Tomato Salad

2 pounds tomatoes (skinned)
1 large onion (finely chopped)
1 heaped tablespoon parsley
  (finely chopped)

Vinaigrette:

¼ pint olive oil
1 level teaspoon salt
½ level teaspoon caster sugar
½ level teaspoon mustard
  powder
4 tablespoons vinegar

SLICE THE TOMATOES and arrange them on a serving dish. Sprinkle on the onion and parsley.

Put the oil, salt, sugar, mustard and vinegar in a small bowl. Whisk thoroughly until it thickens slightly. Pour the vinaigrette over the tomatoes.

Serves 8

Potato Salad

1½ pounds potatoes (cooked)
salt and pepper
2 tablespoons vinaigrette (see page 19)
8 spring onions (chopped)
6 level tablespoons mayonnaise (see page 19)

CHOP THE POTATOES into ½-inch dice and sprinkle with a little salt and pepper and the vinaigrette while still warm. Leave to stand for 30 minutes or until cool. Stir in onions and mayonnaise gently.
Serves 8

Waldorf Salad

3 large red eating apples
4 large sticks celery
6 level teaspoons mayonnaise (see page 19)
1 small lettuce (prepared)
3 ounces walnuts (chopped)

CUT THE UNPEELED apples and celery into ¼-inch dice. Stir in the mayonnaise. Arrange the lettuce leaves on a serving plate and stir the nuts into the salad. Arrange the salad on the leaves and serve at once.
Serves 8

Rice Salad

1 pound Patna rice (cooked)
1 small green pepper (chopped)
1 large eating apple (chopped)
1 large onion (chopped)
8 ounces white grapes
4 ounces flaked almonds (toasted)
salt and pepper
6 heaped tablespoons mayonnaise (see page 19)
4 ounces small firm strawberries (quartered)
2 pineapple rings (chopped)

MIX THE RICE, pepper, apple, onion, grapes and almonds. Season with salt and pepper. Stir in the mayonnaise to moisten and then stir in the strawberries and pineapple. Serve at once.
Serves 8

Nut and Brandy Cream

5-ounce carton double cream
5-ounce carton single cream
2 ounces almond nibs (toasted)
2 tablespoons brandy
ground cinnamon

WHIP THE CREAMS together until they begin to hold their shape. Stir in the nuts and brandy and cinnamon to taste and whip again until the cream is thick enough.
Serves 8

Peaches in Red Wine

8 peaches (slightly under-
   ripe)
¾ pint red wine
2 ounces caster sugar
rind of 1 lemon (thinly pared)
2-inch cinnamon stick
½ ounce arrowroot
½ pint cold water

PEEL THE PEACHES by dropping them first into boiling water for 2 minutes then into cold water for 1 minute. Remove the skins. The skins won't remove easily by this method if the peaches are hard. In this case, peel thinly using a sharp knife, trying to keep each peach round and smooth and free from ridges and corners. Arrange the peaches in a saucepan just large enough for them to fit in one layer. Pour over the red wine. Sprinkle on the sugar, add the lemon rind and the cinnamon. Bring gently to the boil then simmer until the peaches are soft, turning them in the wine if not quite covered.

Remove the peaches on to a serving dish. Blend the arrowroot with a little of the cold water. Use the rest to make the strained wine up to 1 pint. Bring to the boil, pour a little on to the arrowroot then return to the pan, stirring. Bring to the boil again and stir for 2 minutes while the sauce cooks, thickens and clears. Pour over the peaches and chill before serving. Serve with nut and brandy cream (see page 20).

Serves 8

Cheesecake Flan

2 ounces cornflakes (crushed)
2 ounces butter (melted)
8 ounces cottage cheese
1 large lemon
1 packet lemon jelly
2 ounces double cream
2 ounces caster sugar

Decoration:

2 ounces sultanas
rum essence
1 tablespoon cold water

MIX THE CORNFLAKES with the butter and press the mixture into an 8-inch flan tin, pushing it well into the corners to form a flan case. Leave to set for about 1 hour in the fridge. Blend the cottage cheese. Finely grate the rind from the lemon and squeeze out and strain the juice. Make up the lemon jelly to exactly ½ pint, stirring until it has dissolved. When it has cooled, pour it into the blender with the lemon rind and juice, cream and sugar. Blend until smooth. Pour into the case and return to the fridge to set.

Put the sultanas, a few drops of rum essence to taste and the cold water in a small pan. Heat gently until the sultanas are plump. Allow to cool. Drain off excess liquid and use sultanas to decorate the cheesecake.

Serves 8

Caribbean Orange Flowers

8 large oranges
4 ounces sultanas
1 ounce desiccated coconut
2 tablespoons rum
2 tablespoons cold water
juice of 1 lemon (strained)
½ level teaspoon ground allspice
2 ounces soft brown sugar

USING A SHARP knife, cut the rind of each orange into 8 sections, but do not cut right off; leave the rind joined at the base. Cut each section and pith away from the orange flesh, then fold the tip of each rind section underneath the orange to form 8 folded orange leaves. Gently open out the orange flesh segments. Mix the sultanas and coconut and divide between the oranges, pushing the fruit between the segments. Stand each orange on a piece of foil large enough to form a parcel and retain the syrup.

Put the rum, water, lemon juice, allspice and soft brown sugar in a small pan. Heat gently until the sugar dissolves, then boil for about 3 minutes or until syrupy. Pour over the oranges and bake for about 20 minutes at Gas 3/325°F. Unwrap the foil and serve hot or cold. *Serves 8*

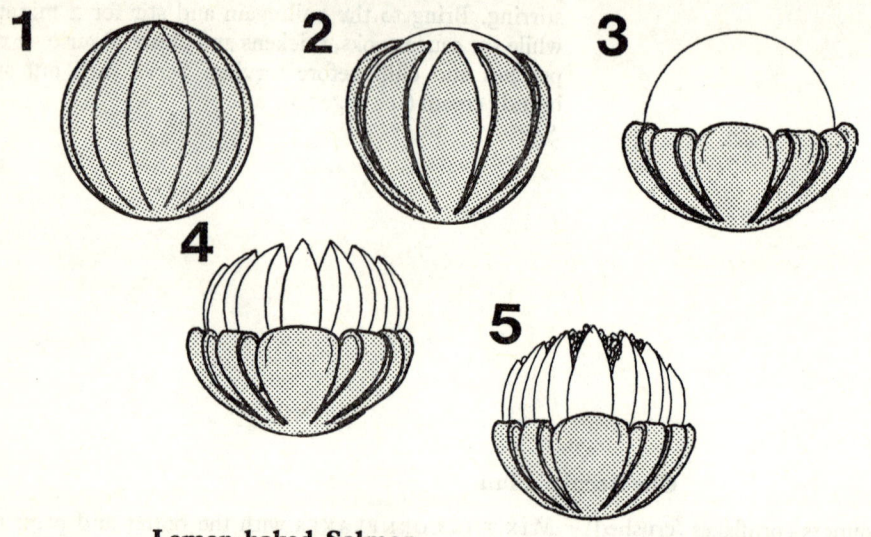

Lemon-baked Salmon

8 salmon steaks
salt and pepper
2 lemons
parsley sprigs

CAREFULLY WIPE STEAKS, removing fins if necessary. Lay each steak on a separate piece of foil large enough to fold into a parcel round the fish. Season steaks with salt and pepper. Squeeze and strain juice from ½ lemon. Pour a little over each steak and add a parsley sprig.

Fold foil pieces into neat parcels to seal in the juices and place on a large baking sheet. Cook for 20–25 minutes, depending on thickness of salmon steaks, at Gas 4/350°F. Slice the whole lemon. Cut the ½ lemon into wedges. Carefully arrange the salmon steaks on a large serving plate. Garnish with the lemon slices and wedges and serve with sauce verte (see page 19). *Serves 8*

Mediterranean Fish Salad

2 pounds haddock
1 large onion (chopped)
2-inch strip lemon rind
2 bay leaves
12 black peppercorns
¼ pint olive oil
juice of 2 lemons (strained)
salt and pepper
parsley (finely chopped)

PUT THE HADDOCK in a large saucepan with the onion, lemon rind, bay leaves and peppercorns. Cover with cold water. Cover and bring to the boil, then simmer for 15 minutes. Don't overcook because the fish will break up too much for this salad. Drain carefully and allow fish to cool.

Whisk oil and lemon juice until it thickens slightly. Season with salt and pepper. Roughly flake the fish when cold and arrange it on a serving plate. Pour over the dressing and sprinkle with parsley.

Serves 8

Onion Quiches

12 ounces plain flour
salt and pepper
3 ounces lard
3 ounces margarine
4 large onions (sliced)
1 ounce butter
1 tablespoon cooking oil
¼ pint milk
¼ pint double cream
4 large eggs (beaten)

SIFT THE FLOUR with a pinch of salt, then rub in the lard and margarine and mix to a stiff dough with cold water. Roll the pastry on a lightly floured board and use to line eight 4-inch fluted tartlet tins. Leave the tins in the fridge to rest.

Separate the onion slices into rings. Heat the butter and oil and fry the onion until soft but not coloured. Allow to cool. Divide the onion between the tartlet tins. Whisk the milk, cream and eggs with salt and pepper. Strain over the onion and bake for about 20 minutes at Gas 6/400°F. then for about 10 minutes at Gas 4/350°F. or until the filling has risen and is golden brown. Allow to cool, then remove from the tins.

Serves 8

Crab Horns

8-ounce packet frozen puff
  pastry
1 small egg (beaten)
4 level tablespoons mayonnaise (see page 19)
4 level tablespoons soured
  cream
salt and pepper
lemon juice (strained)
6 ounces fresh crabmeat
watercress sprigs

ALLOW THE PASTRY to thaw at room temperature for at least 1 hour. Roll the pastry to a rectangle, 10 inches by 12 inches. Cut into ten 1-inch wide strips. Brush one edge of each strip with egg then roll the pastry round cream horn tins, starting at the pointed end. Make sure the egged strip faces inwards and overlaps the pastry spiral so that it will stick. Arrange the horns with the ends underneath on pastry sheets sprinkled with cold water. Bake for about 10 minutes at Gas 7/425°F. until the pastry is golden brown and flaky. Allow to cool for several minutes, then gently twist the tins and remove. Cool the cases completely.

Whisk the mayonnaise, soured cream, salt and pepper and lemon juice to taste. Stir in the crabmeat gently so it doesn't break up too much. Use to fill the horns. Garnish with sprigs of watercress.

Serves 10

Glazed Gammon

5-pound piece gammon hock
2 large onions (skinned)
2 large carrots (peeled)
1 large bay leaf
6 peppercorns
whole cloves
4 level tablespoons Demerara
  sugar
15-ounce can pineapple rings
2 ounces flaked almonds
  (toasted)

WIPE THE MEAT and put it in a large saucepan. Cover with cold water and bring to the boil. Pour off this water, cover with fresh cold water and add the onions, carrots, bay leaf and peppercorns. Bring to the boil slowly, taking off any scum that forms. Time the cooking from the moment the water comes to the boil. Simmer for 1 hour. Drain off the water and put the gammon wrapped in foil into a roasting tin. Bake for 30 minutes at Gas 4/350°F., then remove from the oven and unwrap the foil. Take off the rind and score the fat into diamond shapes. Push a whole clove into the centre of each diamond and sprinkle the fat with the sugar.

Return gammon to the oven for another 30 minutes or until it is crisp and golden. Allow to cool completely and serve on a large board, ready for carving, surrounded by the pineapple rings and sprinkled with the almonds. Cut your own ham frill from plain or greaseproof paper and cellotape it in place round the bone.
Serves 12

Sweet and Sour Pork

¾ pound lean leg of pork
salt and pepper
2 tablespoons soy sauce
¼ pint sherry
7 ounces plain flour
1 standard egg (beaten)
1 pint cold water
peanut oil for deep frying
1 small carrot (peeled)
3-inch piece cucumber
5 tablespoons brown vinegar
3 level tablespoons dark
  brown sugar
2 level tablespoons tomato
  ketchup
2 level tablespoons cornflour

CUT THE MEAT into ½-inch cubes. Mix a pinch each of salt and pepper with the soy sauce and sherry. Pour over the meat and leave to marinate for 30 minutes. Make a batter with 6 ounces flour, egg and ½ pint cold water. Stir in 1 teaspoon peanut oil. Leave to stand for 20 minutes.

Cut the carrot and unpeeled cucumber into matchstick pieces. Sprinkle with a pinch of salt and leave for 5 minutes. Press out liquid. Sprinkle again with a pinch of salt and 2 teaspoons vinegar.

Drain meat, toss in remaining flour to coat, then drop into the batter. Allow excess to drip off, then deep fry in hot peanut (or other vegetable) oil for about 10 minutes or until golden brown. Drain on crumpled kitchen paper and keep hot.

Meanwhile, add 6 tablespoons peanut oil, the remaining vinegar, brown sugar and tomato ketchup to the marinade. Blend the cornflour with ½ pint cold water and stir it in. Bring to the boil, stirring all the time until thick. Add the carrot and cucumber matchsticks and simmer for 2 minutes. Remove and pour immediately over the pork.
Serves 8

Canapés

HOME-MADE CANAPES like these examples are quite
different from the kind most of us have experienced at
cocktail parties. It is much easier for a hostess to keep
crisp ones crisp, chilled ones cold and hot ones hot and
though they are fairly time-consuming to make, canapés
offer lots of scope for imagination. Instead of recipes
here are notes of the various ingredients which can be
used most successfully.

Bases:
1. Various shapes of white and brown bread cut out
   with shaped cutters. Use medium sliced bread and
   keep the shapes fairly small, otherwise they fold with
   the weight of the topping when picked off a tray.
2. Various white and brown bread shapes deep fried
   until they are crisp and golden. Use good vegetable
   oil, drain the shapes well on crumpled kitchen paper
   and store in an airtight tin for two days at the most.
   These shapes can be larger than those described
   above.
3. Pastry cases of all shapes—boats, tartlets, plain and
   fluted.
4. Flat pastry shapes using fairly large cutters; plain
   or fluted. Use plain shortcrust pastry, cheese pastry,
   oatmeal pastry and curry-flavoured pastry for
   variation.
5. Toast cut into fingers and other shapes.
6. Savoury biscuits of all shapes and sizes.

Savoury butters:
These can simply be used as a spread to hold other
toppings to the base, or they can be used on their own,
when they should be piped on the bases.
Soften 4 ounces butter by beating well and add one of the
following:
Curry—2 level teaspoons curry powder
Horseradish—2 level tablespoons creamed horseradish
   sauce
Onion—2 level tablespoons very finely chopped onion
   or shallot
Sardine—4 sardines mashed to a paste
Anchovy—4 fillets mashed to a paste
Blue cheese—2 ounces soft blue cheese
Parsley—2 level tablespoons finely chopped parsley
Watercress—2 ounces finely chopped watercress
Tomato—2 level teaspoons tomato purée.

Cream cheeses:

Use in the same way as the savoury butters.

Soften 4 ounces cream cheese or curd cheese and add one of the following:

Chives—1 rounded tablespoon chopped chives

Tuna—3 level tablespoons tuna, finely mashed with 1 level tablespoon mayonnaise

Ham—1 ounce minced or very finely chopped ham.

Toppings and decorations:

Meat—thin slices of cold meat (beef, lamb, pork, chicken, ham, tongue, salami, luncheon meat etc.) either flat or rolled or formed into cornet shapes, pâté and meat pastes, bacon rolls, salt beef, small sausages

Fish—small whole fish such as sardines or flaked fish or slices of smoked salmon, anchovy fillets, crab and lobster meat, shrimps and prawns

Eggs—hard-boiled and then sliced, quartered or finely chopped and mixed with a little mayonnaise or sandwich spread

Cheese—slices or grated

Salad—small leaves of lettuce, watercress, mustard and cress or really fresh spinach

Tomato—slices or quarters

Cucumber—thin slices, skinned or not as you prefer (or as your canapé colour scheme dictates) arranged flat or formed into cones. Savoury butters or cheeses can be piped into cucumber cones

Beetroot—slices or diced

Asparagus—spears

Onion—rings, raw or deep-fried in batter until crisp, but only if small

Fruit—orange or grapefruit segments, pineapple cubes, apple slices, grapes, lychees and so on

Dried fruit—plumped raisins or sultanas using water, fruit juices or alcohol to do this

Nuts—whole, flaked or nibbed, plain or toasted

Herbs—parsley and mint sprigs, chopped chives, sprigs of thyme, marjoram or any other fresh herb

Olives—black or green or stuffed, whole, halved or sliced when stuffed.

Mushroom Fritters

4 ounces plain flour (sifted)
pinch salt
1 tablespoon cooking oil
¼ pint tepid water
1 standard egg white (whisked)
8 large mushrooms or 16
  small ones
oil or fat for deep frying
lemon wedges

MAKE A WELL in the flour, sprinkle in the salt and add the oil and water. Beat well until smooth. Fold in the whisked egg white and use at once.

Dip each mushroom into the batter and deep fry until golden brown. Drain well on crumpled kitchen paper and serve at once with lemon wedges.
Serves 4

Gazpacho

2 pounds tomatoes (skinned)
2 large onions (chopped)
2 green peppers (chopped)
2 garlic cloves (chopped)
4 tablespoons vinegar
¼ pint olive oil
salt and pepper
2 pints tomato juice
4 tablespoons lemon juice
  (strained)

Croûtons:

4 slices white bread
vegetable oil

SLICE THE TOMATOES, reserving 1 tomato for garnish. Reserve ¼ of the onion and pepper for garnish. Put the vegetables for the soup in a blender with the garlic, vinegar, olive oil, salt, pepper, tomato juice and lemon juice. Blend (in batches if necessary) until smooth. Check the seasoning and pour into a serving bowl. Leave to chill for 30 minutes.

Scoop pips from reserved tomato and chop flesh. Put reserved onion, pepper and tomato into separate bowls.

To make the croûtons, cut crusts off bread and cut bread into ½-inch dice. Fry in vegetable oil until crisp and golden brown, stirring frequently. Drain well and allow to cool. Put in a fourth small bowl. Serve all garnishes with the soup.
Serves 8–12

Chilled Watercress Soup

2 bunches watercress
1 small onion (sliced thinly)
12 ounces potatoes (sliced)
2 ounces butter
1 chicken stock cube
boiling water
½ pint milk
salt and pepper
ground nutmeg
¼ pint double cream

WASH AND DRY watercress by shaking. Trim off coarse roots. Reserve a few good leaves for garnish. Gently fry the onion and potato slices in the butter for about 3 minutes. Dissolve the stock cube in 1 pint boiling water; pour into the pan with the milk. Season with salt, pepper and nutmeg. Simmer gently for 20 minutes. Add the watercress and simmer for a further 10 minutes.

Blend the soup to a smooth purée, cool and then chill in the fridge for at least 1 hour. Just before serving stir the cream into the soup and garnish with the reserved watercress leaves.
Serves 6

Chicken with Almonds

12 chicken drumsticks
seasoned flour
1 large egg (beaten)
4 ounces ground almonds
2 ounces butter
2 ounces flaked almonds
  (toasted)

COAT THE DRUMSTICKS with seasoned flour, then brush with the egg. Dip in ground almonds to coat completely, pressing the almonds well on to the chicken. Melt the butter in a roasting dish and bake the chicken for about 40 minutes at Gas 6/400°F. Baste them once or twice during the roasting. Sprinkle them with the toasted almonds to serve.

Serves 12

2

Dinner Parties

DINNER PARTIES MAY be given for four people to four hundred or more—though I would recommend that one for this latter number be left entirely to the professional caterers. Your dinner parties will depend exactly on how many people your dining table will seat comfortably. Eight is my favourite, it being the largest number for a dinner party one can cope with comfortably on one's own. Dinner parties can be informal or very formal and if the latter is the case you may tell your guests quite subtly by writing a formal little note of invitation.

Once you've decided on the number of people you'll invite and accordingly invited them, it's worth taking their likes and dislikes (if known) into consideration. I don't think it's fair of a guest to arrive and then say he's a vegetarian or that he only eats fish when you've blown the week's housekeeping on a piece of beef. But if you know in advance you can plan your menu to suit everyone.

The table should be set quite early in the morning if possible, or, if it's being used for other meals, early in the afternoon. This is one job which can be got out of the way well in advance and always makes me feel calm once done. Left to the last minute it seems to cause endless trouble. Decide early whether you'll use a tablecloth or tablemats on a polished surface. If you use tablemats, you'll want to provide small mats for the wine glasses or make sure the individual mats are large enough for the plate, cutlery and wine glass.

The centrepiece is important. You can use candles, or perhaps an oil-lamp, which gives a delightful light and is currently very much in favour. A small arrangement of flowers is usual, though this can be varied with the time of the year, using acorns, dried grasses and leaves in autumn, baubles and tinsel at Christmas, new leaves in spring and full-blown flowers in summer. I use plasticine a lot for these arrangements, sticking candles, flowers and baubles in and covering the plasticine with leaves or small blooms. If flowers are in short supply, one beautiful rose in a brandy glass will do wonderfully. Or you might like to slip one flower head into each napkin on the side plate. In Tunisia, they wind trailing leaves in and around each person's plate and cutlery, placing blossoms here and there. This would make a good table arrangement for a summer garden party.

Wine, if you're serving it, should be thought about early. White wine should be chilled in the fridge, put in (unopened) in the morning, and not stuffed hurriedly in the ice-making compartment or freezer at the last moment. Similarly, red wine should be opened at least one hour before it's to be drunk to give it time to 'breathe'. *Don't* dunk it in hot water. It won't do the wine any good at all. Even inexpensive wines benefit from being treated with consideration. Beaujolais breaks the rules and is nicest drunk chilled, particularly the Nouveau Beaujolais which is not allowed to leave the cellars in France until one month after the vintage but then is rushed into the country as soon as possible. If you like the idea of this little ritual, why not give a Nouveau Beaujolais party, choosing your menu to complement this fresh young wine?

It's fun to decant red wine, more so if it's very cheap—a glass decanter on your dinner table looks very special. If your red wine is good and has thrown a sediment, decant it very carefully, leaving the sediment in the bottle. You can always strain this small amount of wine and use it for Russian lamb in wine sauce (see page 31) or peaches in red wine (see page 31). If you're going to sit at the dinner table and not move for coffee, provide half a bottle of wine for each person. The longer one sits and chats the more wine one drinks. Of course you can always end this by not producing another bottle of wine or by serving coffee and petits fours or mints.

Good coffee is essential and instant coffee can be good, provided it's made correctly. Serve it well, from a jug, with heated milk or cream and either plain sugar or coffee crystals, if you like them. Dinner parties can be as simple as you like—just another couple for a homely three-course meal. Or you can serve four courses by providing cheese either before the pudding or with coffee to follow.

When money is short entertaining tends to be put to one side. But there are menus which are really nice, don't cost more than a meal for the family and mean you can keep on seeing your friends yet economise at the same time. Home-made soups can be put on the table for pence and pasta is one of the cheapest ways I know of providing good fare without looking as if you're trying to save money. Toss tagliatelle or noodles in a little double cream, sprinkle it with lots of black pepper and serve it for a filling starter which everyone will enjoy. Spaghetti Bolognese (with a meat sauce) or Milanese (just tomato sauce, no meat) makes a substantial main course and without meat it's very cheap. Breast of lamb, with the excess

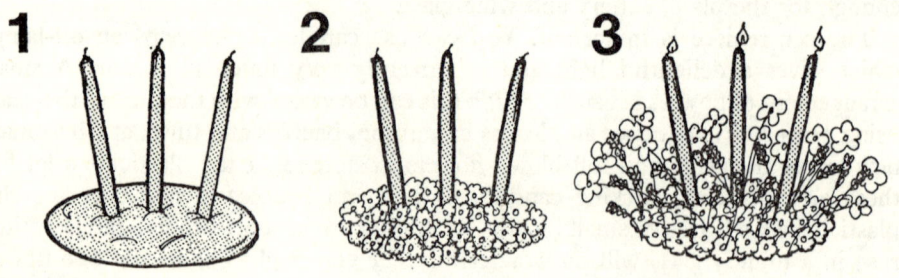

Table Centre
1. Push 3 candles into plasticine. 2. Cover plasticine by sticking on flower heads. 3. Complete the arrangement with longer flowers and leaves.

fat cut away, stuffed and rolled and roasted until the fat is crisp makes another good main course. Casseroles can be made with the cheapest cuts of meat the butcher sells and the addition of a can of tomatoes and their juice and a few herbs brings the casserole into the 'posh' class. Puddings of the mousse sort made with cottage cheese and packet jellies can be made to look special by pouring the mixture into individual dishes and adding a simple decoration. Tinned fruit, heated in its own juice and jazzed up with spices, dried fruit or nuts makes another cheap pud. And nothing beats a good crumble or apple pie if it's home-made and contains fruit from the garden.

Country Pâté

1 pound pig's liver
½ pound green back bacon rashers
1 small onion (chopped)
4 ounces mushrooms (chopped)
2 ounces butter
½ level teaspoon black pepper
½ level teaspoon ground mace
pinch ground nutmeg
4 ounces streaky bacon rashers (stretched)

WASH LIVER AND cut into chunks. Remove bacon rinds and fry them gently until the fat runs. Add the onion and fry for about 5 minutes. Add mushrooms. Roughly chop the back rashers. Mince the liver, bacon, mushrooms and onion twice, though this pâté is best if not too smooth. Turn into a bowl.

Melt the butter and add to the bowl with the pepper, mace and nutmeg. Line a 1-pound loaf tin with the streaky bacon. Turn the mixture into the tin carefully and cook for 1½ hours at Gas 3/325°F. or until slightly shrunk away from the edges.

Serves 8

Russian Lamb in Wine Sauce

1½ pounds boned leg of lamb (sliced)
1 pint lamb stock (made from bones)
1 large carrot (peeled)
1 large onion (skinned)
salt
5 peppercorns
1 bay leaf
1 ounce butter
½ ounce plain flour
1 sugar lump
juice of ½ lemon (strained)
¼ pint dry red wine
1 egg yolk

ASK YOUR BUTCHER to bone the leg of lamb and cut the meat into ⅜-inch thick slices. Make lamb stock from the bones and trimmings. Arrange the lamb slices in a large saucepan. Cover with the stock and bring to the boil. Pour off stock, strain and return to the meat with the carrot and onion. Add salt, peppercorns and bay leaf and simmer for 2 hours or until tender.

Melt the butter in another pan; stir in the flour and remove from the heat. Strain meat stock from meat and measure ½ pint. Gradually stir this stock into the roux. Return to the heat, bring to the boil, stirring all the time and cook gently for about 5 minutes, stirring occasionally. Stir in sugar, lemon juice and wine and allow to cool to hand-hot. Stir in the egg yolk, heat the sauce but do not let it boil, then pour over the meat and serve with noodles tossed in a little butter.

Serves 6

*Buffet party with Glazed
Gammon (page 24) as the main
dish and Tomato Salad (page 19),
Potato Salad (page 20), Rice
Salad (page 20) and Waldorf
Salad (page 20) as
accompaniments. Complete the
spread with Peaches in Red
Wine (page 21) served with Nut
and Brandy Cream (page 20)*

Gingered Cream

5-ounce carton double cream
5-ounce carton single cream
2 pieces preserved ginger
1 tablespoon ginger syrup

WHIP THE CREAMS together until they begin to hold soft peaks. Cut the preserved ginger into tiny pieces and stir it into the creams with the ginger syrup. Continue to whisk until the cream will hold a peak properly.
Serves 8

Potatoes Anna

3½ ounces butter
1½ pounds old potatoes
  (sliced)
salt and pepper

THICKLY BUTTER A round 6-inch cake tin with a fixed base or a 6-inch soufflé dish. Wash the potatoes and dry them in a tea towel. Layer the potato slices in the tin or dish and spread each layer with butter and sprinkle with salt and pepper. The top layer should be butter. Cover lightly with foil and cook for about 1 hour at Gas 5/375°F. Add a little more butter if the potatoes begin to look dry towards the end of the cooking time.
  Turn out of the dish to serve.
Serves 4

French Onion Soup

1½ ounces butter
1 tablespoon olive oil
1½ pounds onions (sliced)
salt and pepper
1 level teaspoon caster sugar
1½ ounces plain flour
2 beef stock cubes
2 pints boiling water
½ pint dry white wine
French bread rounds
  (toasted)
4 ounces Parmesan cheese
  (grated)

HEAT THE BUTTER and oil in a large pan and fry the onions for about 15 minutes over a low heat with the saucepan covered. Stir occasionally to make sure they don't catch on the bottom. Stir in 1 level teaspoon salt and the sugar, raise the heat and cook for about 30 minutes, stirring frequently, until the onions have turned a rich golden brown.
  Sprinkle in the flour and cook for 3 minutes, stirring all the time. Dissolve the stock cubes in the boiling water and gradually add to the pan with the wine. Season with salt and pepper. Simmer for about 45 minutes. Place the toast in the bottom of a tureen; pour on the soup and sprinkle toast with the cheese when it rises.
Serves 6-8

*Serve Little Fish Pies (below)
for a dinner party with Jade
Green Salad (page 34) and
Garlic Cream Dressing (page 36)
For a dessert, Cinnamon Plum
Lattice (page 38)*

French Leeks

1½ pounds leeks
4 tablespoons olive oil
1 garlic clove (chopped)
1 bay leaf
2 large tomatoes (skinned)
salt and pepper
1 teaspoon lemon juice
  (strained)

WASH LEEKS THOROUGHLY and cut into 1-inch lengths. Heat the oil in a large frying-pan. Add the leeks, garlic and bay leaf and cook slowly for 20 minutes, covering the pan. Chop the tomatoes. Add the tomatoes to the pan with salt and pepper and cook for a further 5 minutes until the leeks are tender but still fairly crisp. Stir in the lemon juice and serve at once.
Serves 4

Ratatouille

1 large aubergine (sliced)
1 large courgette (sliced)
3 large tomatoes (skinned)
4 tablespoons olive oil
1 small onion (chopped)
1 garlic clove (chopped)
1 small green pepper
  (chopped)
salt and pepper

PUT THE AUBERGINE and courgette slices in a colander and put a plate on top with a weight to press out excess water. Leave for 30 minutes. Chop the tomatoes.

Heat the oil in a large frying-pan. Add the onion and garlic and fry until soft but not coloured. Add the aubergine, courgette, tomato and green pepper and fry gently for 30 minutes, adding more olive oil if necessary. Season well with salt and pepper.
Serves 4

Sherried Grapefruit

2 large grapefruit
2 ounces Demerara sugar
4 dessertspoons sherry (dry
  or sweet)
4 glacé cherries

CUT THE GRAPEFRUIT in half. Using a sharp knife, cut round the fruit between the flesh and the pith, then separate each segment. Sprinkle each half with the sugar and 1 dessertspoon of sherry. Grill under a hot grill for 3 minutes or until golden brown. Serve hot, with a glacé cherry for decoration.
Serves 4

Little Fish Pies

1½ pounds cod (cooked)
salt and pepper
8-ounce packet frozen peas
3 ounces butter
1 ounce plain flour
2 ounces mushrooms
¾ pint milk
1½ pounds potato (cooked)
1 level tablespoon parsley
  (finely chopped)

FLAKE THE COD and season it with salt and pepper. Stir in the peas. Melt 1 ounce butter in a saucepan. Stir in the flour and cook gently for 2 minutes. Melt 1 ounce butter in another pan. Leave mushrooms whole if small, otherwise halve or quarter. Cook gently for 4 minutes, stirring occasionally. Gradually stir all but 4 tablespoons milk into the flour mixture in the pan. Bring to the boil, stirring all the time and cook gently for 3 minutes. Season well with salt and pepper. Drain the mushrooms and stir into the sauce. Stir in the fish and peas and

2

divide the mixture between 6 small ovenproof dishes. Mash the potato with the remaining milk and butter and stir in the parsley. Pipe the potato over each pie and then cook for 35 minutes at Gas 4/350°F.
Serves 6

Chocolate Sauce

1 level tablespoon cornflour
1 level tablespoon cocoa
1 level dessertspoon caster sugar
½ pint milk
½ ounce butter
2 ounces sultanas
1 tablespoon rum

BLEND THE CORNFLOUR and cocoa with the sugar and 1 tablespoon of the milk. Heat the remainder of the milk with the butter. Soak the sultanas in the rum. Pour a little of the hot milk on the blended cocoa, stir well and return cocoa to the saucepan. Bring to the boil, stirring all the time while the sauce thickens and cooks. Cook for a further 2 minutes. Stir in the rum-flavoured sultanas at the last moment.
Serves 6

Chocolate Soufflé

1 ounce butter
1 ounce plain flour
¼ pint milk
1½ ounces plain chocolate
1 ounce caster sugar
3 large eggs (separated)
chocolate sauce (see above)

MELT THE BUTTER in a saucepan. Stir in the flour and cook the mixture gently for about 3 minutes. Heat the milk and chocolate until the chocolate dissolves. Gradually, stir the milk mixture into the pan, making sure the sauce is smooth. Bring to the boil, stirring all the time until the mixture is very thick. Stir in the sugar and allow to cool slightly.

Add the egg yolks to the mixture one at a time, beating well after each one. Whisk the whites until stiff. Fold them into the chocolate mixture and turn the mixture into a greased 7-inch soufflé dish. Bake for about 35 minutes at Gas 6/400°F. or until well risen and brown. Serve at once with chocolate sauce.
Serves 6

Jade Green Salad

2 green eating apples (chopped)
1 large avocado pear (chopped)
juice of 1 lemon (strained)
4 sticks celery (chopped)
watercress (washed)
mustard and cress (washed)
lettuce (washed)
½ cucumber (chopped)
4 ounces walnuts (chopped)

PUT THE APPLES and avocado pear in a serving bowl. Pour on the lemon juice and toss to coat well. Add the celery, watercress, mustard and cress, lettuce and cucumber. Toss well. Sprinkle on the nuts and serve with garlic cream dressing (see page 36).
Serves 8

Butter-glazed Carrots

1 pound carrots (scraped)
1 ounce butter
good pinch caster sugar
salt and pepper
1 heaped teaspoon mint
  (finely chopped)

LEAVE THE CARROTS whole if new or, if using old carrots, peel them and cut them into 1–inch lengths. Melt the butter in a saucepan. Add the carrots, sugar and salt and pepper. Cover with water and bring to the boil. Simmer very slowly, shaking the pan occasionally, to prevent the carrots catching on the bottom. Cook for about 30 minutes. Serve with a little of the remaining liquid poured over the carrots. Sprinkle with the mint.
Serves 4

Flamed Mushrooms

2 garlic cloves (chopped)
1 small onion (chopped)
2 ounces butter
2 pounds mushrooms (sliced)
2 teaspoons lemon juice
  (strained)
1 level teaspoon caster sugar
4 tablespoons brandy
1 pint double cream
salt and pepper

COOK THE GARLIC and onion in the butter for 5 minutes or until soft but not browned. Add the mushrooms with the lemon juice and sugar and cook for about 6 minutes, then steam off any remaining moisture. Add brandy and flame. Pour in the cream and seasoning and cook gently, stirring, until thickened. Serve with toast croûtons.
Serves 8

Herbed Guard of Honour

2 pieces best end neck of
  lamb (each with 7 or 8
  cutlets)
5 level teaspoons mustard
  powder
6 tablespoons white wine
4 tablespoons single cream
3 level teaspoons mixed herbs
½ level teaspoon thyme
½ pint lamb stock
4 level teaspoons plain flour
salt and pepper
1 teaspoon lemon juice
  (strained)

ASK YOUR BUTCHER to prepare the two pieces of meat for a guard of honour, scraping the ends of the bones clean. With the meat facing, interleave the bones like a wedding guard of honour. You may have to secure the meat with string to hold it during the cooking. Cook for 10 minutes at Gas 8/450°F. then reduce to Gas 4/350°F. and cook for 5 minutes more. Cover the scraped bones with foil to keep them white during the remainder of the cooking. Lightly score the meat. Mix 4 level teaspoons mustard with 2 tablespoons wine and 2 tablespoons cream. Add 2 teaspoons herbs and the thyme. Spread this mixture over the meat and into the cuts. Cook for 1 hour 45 minutes more spreading with rest of herb mixture until used.

Mix remaining mustard, wine, cream and herbs. Add stock. Pour 3 tablespoons cooking juices from meat into a pan and stir in the flour. Add stock and bring to the boil. Cook for 5 minutes, stirring frequently. When smooth and not too thick, season and add lemon juice. Cut string off meat and put a cutlet frill on each bone end.
Serves 8

Garlic Cream Dressing

1 level teaspoon caster sugar
2 ounces warm water
1 level teaspoon Dijon
  mustard
1 garlic clove (crushed)
salt and pepper
2 tablespoons oil
2 teaspoons vinegar
4 tablespoons double cream

DISSOLVE THE SUGAR in the water. Stir in the mustard. Beat in the garlic, seasoning, oil and vinegar. Beat well. Beat in the cream.
Serves 8

Vichyssoise

4 ounces butter
8 large leeks (chopped)
2 large onions (chopped)
salt and pepper
4 medium potatoes (chopped)
4 chicken stock cubes
3½ pints boiling water
½ pint double cream
parsley (finely chopped)

MELT THE BUTTER in a large saucepan and fry the leeks and onions gently for about 10 minutes or until soft but not browned. Add salt and pepper and the potatoes. Dissolve the chicken stock cubes in the boiling water and pour into the pan. Bring to boiling point, then simmer for about 40 minutes. Blend the soup until smooth.

Stir the cream into the soup and leave to chill in the fridge for 2 hours. Serve sprinkled with the parsley.
Serves 8

Cucumber Salad

2 cucumbers (peeled)
salt and pepper
vinaigrette (see page 19)
parsley (chopped)

SLICE THE CUCUMBER wafer-thin and coat each layer well with salt as you arrange it in a basin. Leave for 1 hour, preferably longer. Rinse very thoroughly to remove all traces of salt. By this time the cucumber should be limp. Drain well. Toss in vinaigrette dressing, sprinkle with pepper and parsley and chill before serving.
Serves 8

After-Dinner Mints

1 pound icing sugar (sifted)
1 teaspoon glycerine
2 standard egg whites (beaten)
oil of peppermint
green colouring
4 ounces plain chocolate

PUT THE ICING sugar in a basin and add the glycerine and a little egg white. Knead to a firm consistency, adding more egg white as necessary. Add a few drops of peppermint and colour pale green. Roll mixture to ¼-inch thickness and cut out rounds using a 1½-inch cutter. Leave on baking sheets to harden.

Melt the chocolate in a basin over a pan of hot water. Dip each peppermint in the chocolate to cover half, or drop in completely if liked. Take out with a palette knife and leave to dry on lightly greased baking sheets.
Makes 30

Tagliatelle with Cream

1 pound tagliatelle
salt and pepper
½ pint double cream

COOK THE TAGLIATELLE in plenty of fast-boiling salted water for about 10 minutes or until it is soft but still has a slightly nutty bite when tasted. Drain well and stir in the double cream, tossing the pasta to coat completely. Sprinkle with pepper, freshly ground black pepper if possible, and serve.
Serves 8

Croquette Potatoes

2 pounds potatoes (cooked)
2 ounces butter
2 large eggs (beaten)
1 level tablespoon parsley (chopped)
salt and pepper
plain flour
browned breadcrumbs
oil or fat for deep frying

MASH THE POTATOES with the butter and 1 egg until really smooth. Mix in the parsley and salt and pepper to taste. Form the mixture into small balls or rolls, using your hands and flouring them each time. Coat each ball or roll with egg and then with breadcrumbs; twice helps prevent them breaking during cooking. Fry the croquettes for 4–5 minutes or until golden brown. Drain well on crumpled kitchen paper and serve.
Serves 8

Broccoli with Almonds

1 pound broccoli (prepared)
salt and pepper
4 ounces butter
1½ ounces flaked almonds

COOK THE PREPARED broccoli in boiling salted water for about 15 minutes or until cooked and tender but not mushy. Melt the butter in a frying-pan and gently fry the almonds until golden brown, stirring all the time over a gentle heat. Drain the broccoli, arrange it carefully in a serving dish and pour over the almonds and the butter. Sprinkle with freshly ground black pepper and serve.
Serves 4

Golden Cauliflower

1 medium-sized cauliflower (prepared)
salt and pepper
3 ounces butter
1 garlic clove (crushed)
2 ounces fresh white breadcrumbs

COOK THE CAULIFLOWER in plenty of boiling salted water for about 25 minutes or until tender and cooked but not soft. While the cauliflower cooks, melt the butter in a frying-pan, stir in the crushed clove of garlic and breadcrumbs and stir over a gentle heat until the crumbs are crisp and golden.

Drain the cauliflower well and keep whole. Arrange in a serving dish. Coat with the breadcrumbs and serve at once.
Serves 4

Orange Roast Pork

4-pound piece pork loin
   (chined)
salt and pepper
3 tablespoons cooking oil
rind of 2 large oranges
   (finely grated)
juice of 3 large oranges
   (strained)
3 tablespoons clear honey

ASK YOUR BUTCHER to score the skin in a small and even diamond pattern, or do this yourself using a very sharp small knife. Season the skin with salt and rub the skin with 1 tablespoon cooking oil. Heat the remaining oil in a roasting tin, add the meat and stand first on one end then the other to seal the juices. Stand meat finally with scored skin up. Mix the rind, juice and honey and pour half over the meat. Roast for 2 hours at Gas 5/375°F. then raise heat to Gas 7/425°F. and pour remaining honey and orange mixture over the meat. Roast for about 40 minutes more or until the crackling is really crisp and golden brown.
Serves 8

Round-the-World Kebabs

8 streaky bacon rashers
1 large avocado
2 large bananas
juice of 1 lemon (strained)
16 prawns (peeled)

REMOVE THE BACON rinds and cut the bacon rashers into 1½-inch pieces. Fry gently until the fat runs then cook until almost done, but still soft. Meanwhile, peel the avocado, remove the stone and cut the flesh into even-sized pieces, each about 1 inch across. Peel and cut the bananas into 1-inch slices. Toss the fruit in the lemon juice to coat and prevent browning.

Thread the bacon, avocado, banana and prawns on to kebab sticks. Grill for about 2 minutes until the kebabs turn golden at the edges.
Serves 8

Cinnamon Plum Lattice

8 ounces plain flour
4 level teaspoons ground
   cinnamon
5 ounces soft margarine
2 tablespoons cold water
20-ounce can red plums
1 heaped teaspoon arrowroot
milk
1 heaped teaspoon caster
   sugar

SIFT THE FLOUR and 2 level teaspoons cinnamon into a bowl. Add margarine and water and, using a fork, mix to a stiff dough. Knead lightly on a floured board and roll out and use to line an 8-inch fluted flan ring. Reserve trimmings. Line flan with a piece of grease-proof paper and fill with baking beans. Bake for 15 minutes at Gas 6/400°F. Remove beans and paper and bake for 5 minutes more. Allow to cool then remove flan ring and cool completely on a wire rack.

Drain the plums. Arrange the plums in the flan in a single layer without squashing the fruit into the case. Pour the juice into a small pan. Stir in the remaining cinnamon. Blend the arrowroot with a little cold water. Bring the juice to the boil; stir into the arrowroot and return to pan. Bring to boil, stirring all the time while the sauce thickens and clears. Cook gently for about

2 minutes. Pour over the fruit to glaze. Roll remaining pastry and cut into strips about $\frac{1}{4}$-inch wide. Use to form a lattice sticking them to the pastry case by moistening the ends with water. Brush with milk and bake for about 20 minutes, or until pale golden brown at Gas 5/375°F. Brush again with milk and dust with caster sugar along each strip. Serve hot or cold.
Serves 6

Coffee

2 heaped tablespoons ground coffee

1 pint water

Jug method   Warm the jug, add the coffee and pour on freshly boiling water. Stir and leave to stand for 3 minutes, then skim the surface with a spoon to settle the grounds. Leave for 1 minute more. Using a strainer pour into coffee cups and hand sugar and cream or milk separately.

Saucepan method   Heat the coffee and water together in a saucepan. Bring almost to boiling point. Remove from the heat, stir, cover and leave to stand for 4 minutes. Strain into a warmed jug and serve.

Filter method   Warm the jug and measure the coffee into the filter on top. Pour the water on to the coffee and allow it to subside through the coffee, filtering into the jug below. Don't pour in too much water at any one time.

Percolator method   Pour measured water into percolator and measure coffee into the basket. Put in percolator and put on lid. Percolate for 6–8 minutes, remove basket and serve the coffee. Don't over-percolate as this may spoil the flavour.

Milk   If you want to serve hot milk, heat it almost to boiling point. Boiled milk can impair the flavour of your coffee.
Serves 6

Stuffed Breast of Lamb

2 large breasts of lamb (boned)

2 ounces streaky bacon (chopped)

1 ounce butter

2 large onions (chopped)

1 small green pepper (chopped)

2 large cooking apples (chopped)

ASK YOUR BUTCHER to bone the lamb, or do this yourself with a sharp small knife. Use the bones to make stock for the gravy. Cut off excess fat and lay the meat flat on a board, skin side down. Fry the bacon with the butter in a large frying-pan for 2 minutes. Add the onions and pepper and cook for a further 8 minutes. Stir in the apples, breadcrumbs, parsley, salt and pepper and a pinch of sugar. Add the apricots and mix to a stuffing with the egg. Spread this mixture on the lamb to within $\frac{1}{2}$-inch of the edges and roll each piece

4 ounces fresh white
   breadcrumbs
2 level tablespoons parsley
   (chopped)
salt and pepper
caster sugar
4 ounces dried apricots
   (chopped)
1 large egg (beaten)
1 ounce dripping

separately and not too tightly. Tie in several places with clean thin string. Calculate the weight.

Melt the dripping in a roasting tin and roast the meat for 30 minutes to the pound plus 30 minutes or until the fat on the meat is fairly crisp. Serve cut into thick slices.
Serves 8

Spaghetti Bolognese

2 ounces streaky bacon
   (chopped)
1 small onion (chopped)
1 small carrot (chopped)
1 pound raw minced beef
$\frac{1}{4}$ pint dry red wine
$\frac{1}{2}$ beef stock cube
$\frac{1}{2}$ pint boiling water
1 level tablespoon tomato
   purée
salt and pepper
1 level teaspoon mixed dried
   herbs
1 pound spaghetti
1 ounce butter
Parmesan cheese (grated)

FRY THE BACON in a large frying-pan until the fat begins to run, then add the onion and carrot and fry for about 10 minutes. Stir in the minced meat and cook for 10 minutes, stirring all the time until the meat has browned. Gradually stir in the wine. Dissolve the stock cube in the boiling water and stir the stock into the pan with the tomato purée and salt and pepper and herbs. Bring to the boil, then simmer for 30 minutes.

Cook the spaghetti in plenty of fast-boiling salted water for about 10 minutes. Drain well and toss over the heat in the butter until coated. Turn into a serving dish. Check the seasoning of the meat sauce and pour over the spaghetti. Sprinkle with Parmesan and hand more round separately.
Serves 8

Milanese Sauce

1 small onion (chopped)
2 ounces mushrooms
   (chopped)
1 ounce butter
15-ounce can tomatoes
1 small bay leaf
pinch dried thyme
1 level teaspoon caster sugar
salt and pepper
pinch ground nutmeg
2 ounces ham (cooked)
1 level tablespoon tomato
   purée (optional)

FRY THE ONION and mushrooms in the butter for about 5 minutes. Stir in the tomatoes and their juice, the bay leaf, thyme, sugar, salt, pepper and nutmeg. Bring to the boil, then simmer for 20 minutes, covered.

Cut the ham into small pieces. Add to the pan with the tomato purée, if used, and simmer for another 5 minutes. Serve with any kind of pasta.
Serves 8

Raspberry Cream

1 packet raspberry jelly
15-ounce can raspberries
8 ounces cottage cheese
5-ounce carton double cream
cochineal if necessary
8 fresh strawberries (sliced)

MAKE UP THE raspberry jelly using the juice from the raspberries made up to ½ pint with cold water. Allow to cool, then pour the jelly, raspberries, cottage cheese and double cream into a blender. Blend until smooth, adding a few drops of cochineal if the colour is too pale. Pour into 8 small glasses and leave to set. When set, decorate each one with strawberry slices.
Serves 8

Spiced Oranges

2 8-ounce cans mandarin
    oranges
1 level teaspoon ground
    cinnamon
2 pieces preserved ginger
1 tablespoon ginger syrup
2 ounces almond nibs
2 ounces sultanas
1 tablespoon sweet sherry

PUT THE ORANGES and their juice in a saucepan. Stir in the cinnamon. Cut the preserved ginger into very small pieces and add to the pan with the syrup, nuts, sultanas and sherry. Heat gently until almost at boiling point, then turn into individual dishes. Serve with whipped cream.
Serves 4

Gooseberry Crumble

1½ pounds gooseberries
5 ounces caster sugar
6 ounces plain flour
3 ounces butter
rind of 1 orange (finely
    grated)

TOP AND TAIL the gooseberries and put in an oven-proof dish. Sprinkle with 2 ounces caster sugar and 2 tablespoons cold water. Sift the flour into a bowl. Rub in the butter, stir in the remaining sugar and the orange rind and sprinkle this crumble over the fruit. Press down lightly and smooth the top. Bake for about 40 minutes at Gas 6/400°F. until golden brown. Serve with cream.
Serves 6

Spiced Apple Pie

8 ounces plain flour
pinch salt
2 ounces lard
2 ounces margarine
2 pounds cooking apples
    (sliced)
3 ounces caster sugar
1 level teaspoon ground
    cinnamon
3 ounces raisins
4 tablespoons brandy

SIFT THE FLOUR and salt into a bowl. Rub in the lard and margarine and mix to a stiff dough with cold water. Roll out on a floured board and use half to line an 8-inch pie plate. Cover pastry with the apple slices. Mix the sugar and cinnamon and sprinkle over the fruit. Soak the raisins in the brandy for 30 minutes, then sprinkle over the apples. Cover the pie with the remaining pastry and seal and decorate the edge. If you like, decorate the top with pastry trimmings.

Bake for about 30 minutes at Gas 6/400°F. or until the pastry is golden brown.
Serves 6–8

Beef Casserole

3 pounds shin of beef
3 tablespoons cooking oil
2 garlic cloves (crushed)
1 pound onions (skinned)
1 level tablespoon tomato
    purée
1 large bay leaf
2-inch cinnamon stick
pinch ground cumin
6 tablespoons red wine
3 tablespoons wine vinegar
salt and pepper

CUT THE MEAT into 1-inch cubes and brown on all sides in half the oil in a heatproof casserole. Just cover with water and cook for 1 hour at Gas 3/325°F. Heat the remaining oil in a pan and fry the garlic. Quarter the onions and add to the pan. Stir in the purée, bay leaf, cinnamon, cumin, wine and wine vinegar and salt and pepper to season. Simmer for 5 minutes, then pour into the casserole and continue cooking for another 2 hours. Serve with rice.

Serves 8

Tea Parties

THE VICTORIANS MADE the mid-afternoon into a time of entertaining. On the stroke of 3 o'clock or 4 o'clock depending on the household, the mistress would ring the bell and a succession of upstairs maids, headed by the butler, would appear with all that was required for this most exquisite little meal. The tea itself, served in a silver tea pot with silver hot water jug, milk jug and sugar bowl with tongs for the sugar, wafer-thin sandwiches of favoured varieties and the three-tier cakestand with five or six different kinds of cake, all home-made downstairs by the ruler of the kitchens, the cook. All the food was arranged on doilies made of lace, or sometimes of crochet, and the tea service would be the most beautiful bone china, delicate and semi-transparent, with silver tea knives and cake forks, smaller and daintier than those from the dinner service.

Isn't it a pity that this form of entertaining has fallen out of fashion! I think we should revive it. There are two kinds of tea party. There's the homely, round-the-fire sort when you should serve hot dripping toast, crumpets with lashings of butter, home-made scones with home-made jam or if not, the new fruity conserves (the kind that must be kept in the fridge once opened) and great slabs of fruit cake —again home-made. Tea to drink should be plentiful whether you choose to offer china tea, lemon tea or thick cups of dark, steaming brew.

The dainty tea party, ideal for summer's entertaining, should consist of tiny sandwiches with deliciously moist fillings such as cucumber, salmon or mashed hard-boiled egg moistened with real mayonnaise. Cakes should also be tiny—small sponges cut in fancy shapes from a large round and iced and decorated individually in delicate pastel shades. Serve brandy snaps filled with cream, a gâteau, madeleines, palmiers, those heart-shaped puff pastries sandwiched with cream, tiny meringues and other home-made delicacies.

Coffee Parties
Coffee parties have crossed the Atlantic along with the practice of selling to house-wives in their own homes, though originally the coffee-party custom was taken to

America from the Scandinavian countries by the immigrants of the eighteenth and nineteenth centuries. The differences between a coffee party and a tea party are numerous and worth noting.

Naturally, coffee is served at coffee parties because they take place in the morning rather than the afternoon. No sandwiches or savouries are served; the coffee party gives one a chance to show off one's baking, and cakes and gâteaux, biscuits and tarts are displayed in profusion. Often the goodies are spicey, like many of the cakes and cookies served in the Scandinavian countries even today. Yeast mixtures play a large part in the coffee morning (again a legacy from the colder northern countries) and biscuits of all kinds are served, often variations of the same basic mixture. The freezer can play a large part in coffee-morning entertaining. Many of the cookie mixtures can be formed into a roll, frozen and then sliced from the frozen state and baked. The remainder can be left in the freezer for the next time. Complete gâteaux can be frozen standing on a baking sheet and wrapped when solid, but the wraps must come off before thawing begins or you'll find the papers sticking to cream and chocolate decorations. You'll find instructions for making good coffee on page 39 but in summer iced coffee (page 52) could be served.

Shortbread

3 ounces unsalted butter (softened)
3 ounces plain flour
1 ounce rice flour
1 ounce ground almonds
1½ ounces caster sugar

RUB THE BUTTER into the flour, sprinkling on the rice flour if the butter gets sticky. Stir in the almonds and sugar and spread the mixture in a 6-inch sandwich tin with a loose bottom. Press lightly and make a pattern on the surface. Bake for about 1 hour 15 minutes at Gas 2/300°F. The shortbread should become a pale biscuit colour. Leave to cool in the tin but while still warm, mark into 6 wedges.
Serves 6

Coconut Cake

12 ounces self-raising flour
pinch salt
6 ounces butter
6 ounces caster sugar
4 ounces desiccated coconut
2 large eggs (beaten)
¼ pint milk

SIFT THE FLOUR and salt into a bowl. Rub in the butter. Stir in the sugar and coconut and mix to a stiff dropping consistency with the eggs and as much of the milk as is necessary. Turn the mixture into a greased and lined 7-inch round cake tin.

Bake for about 1½ hours or until well-risen and firm to the touch at Gas 4/350°F. Allow to cool for 15 minutes in the tin, then turn on to a wire rack to finish cooling.

Fruit Tartlets

8 ounces plain flour
pinch salt
2 ounces margarine
2 ounces lard
1 small egg (beaten)
fresh strawberries or
   raspberries
2 heaped tablespoons
   raspberry jam
canned mandarins, apricots,
   cherries or gooseberries
2 level teaspoons arrowroot
whipped cream

SIFT THE FLOUR and salt into a bowl. Rub in the margarine and lard and mix to a stiff dough with the egg and cold water if necessary. Knead the pastry lightly on a floured board and roll out. Use to line four 4-inch fluted tartlet tins. Line each one with greaseproof paper and fill with baking beans. Bake blind for 10 minutes at Gas 5/375°F. Remove paper and beans and bake for 5 minutes more or until golden brown and crisp. Allow to cool on wire racks.

When cold fill with fresh strawberries or raspberries. Heat the raspberry jam in a small saucepan. Allow to cool a little but not set, then spoon it over the fruit to cover completely. Serve the same day.

Or, fill the tartlets with well-drained canned fruit, pouring the juice into a saucepan. Blend the arrowroot with a little cold water. Heat the juice, stir it into the arrowroot, return the mixture to the pan and cook gently for 2 minutes, stirring while the sauce thickens and clears. Pour this glaze over canned fruits. Decorate if liked with whipped double cream, piping stars between the pieces of fruit.

Serves 4

Eclairs

2 ounces lard
¼ pint cold water
2¼ ounces plain flour (sifted)
pinch salt
2 large eggs (beaten)
5-ounce carton double
   cream (whipped)
Chocolate glacé icing:
2 level teaspoons cocoa
2 tablespoons boiling water
6 ounces icing sugar (sifted)

PUT THE LARD and cold water in a pan and bring to the boil. As soon as it boils, quickly add the flour and salt, pull the pan off the heat and beat it thoroughly until the mixture is smooth and glossy and leaves the sides of the pan quite clean. Use a wooden spoon. Allow the mixture to cool until you can stand the pan on the palm of your hand. Beat in the eggs until the mixture is glossy and firm and capable of holding its own shape. Spoon into a piping bag fitted with a large plain nozzle.

Pipe finger lengths on greased baking sheets and bake for about 30 minutes at Gas 7/425°F. Allow to cool on a wire rack. Make a cut in the side of each one and fill with whipped cream. Dissolve the cocoa in the boiling water and gradually beat in the icing sugar to make a smooth coating. Dip the top of each éclair in the icing, swirling as you lift it to catch the drip on top. Allow to dry.

Makes 16

Vanilla Slices

8-ounce packet frozen puff
  pastry
4 ounces raspberry jam
cochineal
Confectioners' custard:
2 large egg yolks
2 ounces caster sugar
¾ ounce plain flour
½ ounce cornflour
½ pint milk
1 large egg white
vanilla essence

Glacé icing:
8 ounces icing sugar (sifted)
2–3 tablespoons warm water

ALLOW THE PASTRY to thaw at room temperature for at least 1 hour. Roll it on a floured board to a 10-inch square. Cut in half. Place both pieces on wet baking sheets and bake for about 25 minutes or until well-risen and golden brown at Gas 8/450°F. Allow to cool. Spread the underside of the best piece of pastry with jam.

Make the confectioners' custard by creaming the egg yolks and sugar until really thick and pale. Beat in the flour and cornflour and a little cold milk to make a smooth paste. Heat the remaining milk almost to boiling point then pour it on to the egg mixture, stirring all the time. Return to the pan and bring to the boil, stirring over a low heat. Cook for about 2 minutes stirring continuously. Whisk the egg white until stiff. Remove the pan from the heat, stir in the egg white and vanilla essence to taste and cook for 1 minute more. Allow to cool completely, then spread over the second pastry half. Sandwich the two pieces together. Stir the icing sugar and 2 tablespoons warm water together for the glacé icing. It should coat the back of the spoon. Add more warm water if too thick.

Colour 1 tablespoon of glacé icing pale pink with cochineal and put this icing into a greaseproof icing bag. Spread the plain glacé icing over the top of the vanilla slice and then pipe pink lines across the top ½ inch apart. Using a skewer, draw lines down the vanilla slice in alternate directions at ½-inch intervals to make the feather pattern. Leave to set, then cut the slice into 6 pieces using a very sharp knife and sawing through the pastry without putting any pressure on it.
Makes 6

Sandwiches

MAKE YOUR SANDWICHES from white bread or brown or wholemeal breads. Leave the granary, poppyseed, black and other loaves for the homely teas round the fire. Cut the bread into thin slices and butter it fairly generously with unsalted or slightly salted butter.

Filling suggestions:
tinned salmon mashed and mixed with a little vinegar
  and pepper
hard-boiled eggs mashed and mixed with seasoning and
  mayonnaise
thinly-sliced cucumber sprinkled with a little vinegar
sardines with bones removed and mashed
smoked salmon sprinkled with a little lemon juice

fish pastes such as shrimp and salmon spread

thinly-sliced ham spread with a little mustard

scrambled egg beaten and mixed with a little very finely chopped onion

lettuce and sandwich spread

tuna fish mashed and mustard and cress

potted meats such as chicken or ham or beef well seasoned

sliced pressed tongue spread with a little mustard

skinned tomatoes, thinly sliced and sprinkled with salt and pepper

Remove the crusts and cut the sandwiches into 4 squares or triangles or, using small fancy cutters, cut out shapes. Sandwich 1 slice brown with 1 slice white and alternate on a tray, first the brown side then the white to look like a chequer board. Arrange all sandwiches on doilies on plates and garnish with mustard and cress, watercress, tomato quarters, parsley sprigs, cucumber cones and lemon slices.

Viennese Cookies

8 ounces butter

2 ounces icing sugar

2 ounces cornflour

6 ounces plain flour

pinch salt

glacé cherries (halved)

angelica leaves

5-ounce carton double cream (whipped)

2 ounces plain chocolate

2 ounces almond nibs (toasted)

CREAM THE BUTTER and icing sugar until soft and smooth. Sift the cornflour, flour and salt and fold into the creamed mixture until it binds together. Spoon into a piping bag and pipe circles and stars on greased baking sheets. Decorate the stars with glacé cherry halves and the circles with diamond-shaped leaves cut from angelica. Pipe even numbers of fingers and shells. Bake for 10–12 minutes at Gas 5/375°F. Cool on wire racks.

Sandwich the shells and fingers together with whipped cream. Melt the chocolate in a small basin standing over a pan of hot water. Dip the shells (either end) into the chocolate then into toasted nuts and leave to set.
Makes 12

Jam and Cream Scones

8 ounces plain flour

2 level teaspoons baking powder

½ level teaspoon salt

2 ounces butter

¼ pint buttermilk

5 rounded tablespoons strawberry jam

5-ounce carton clotted or double cream (lightly whipped)

SIFT THE FLOUR, baking powder and salt into a bowl. Rub in the butter and mix to a soft but not sticky dough using the buttermilk. Turn on to a floured board and knead lightly. Roll to a ½-inch thickness and cut into rounds using a 2½-inch fluted cutter. Bake for 10 minutes at Gas 8/450°F. Cool on a wire rack and serve slightly warm or cold, with the jam and cream.
Makes 10

Chocolate Gâteau

8 ounces self-raising flour
1 level teaspoon salt
8 ounces margarine
8 ounces caster sugar
4 large eggs
1 pound unsalted butter
1 pound icing sugar
3 ounces cocoa
1 pound plain chocolate
crystallised violets

SIFT THE FLOUR and salt into a bowl. Cream the margarine and sugar until fluffy. Beat in the eggs one at a time, beating well after each one. Gradually fold in the flour and turn the mixture into a greased and floured 8-inch round cake tin. Bake for 45–50 minutes or until well-risen and golden brown at Gas 4/350°F. Leave to cool a little in the tin, then turn out on to a wire rack.

Cream 8 ounces butter until really soft. Sift the icing sugar and cocoa together and gradually beat it into the butter. When the cake is cold, cut it into 3 or 4 layers. Sandwich together again with the chocolate butter icing. Put the remaining butter with the chocolate in a large basin standing over a pan of hot water. Allow to melt, then cool and beat until thick enough to spread. Spread over the cake and whirl with a palette knife. Decorate with crystallised violets.

Serves 10–12

Meringue Stars

3 large egg whites
6 ounces caster sugar
cochineal
½ pint double cream

WHISK THE EGG whites until standing in stiff peaks and fluffy without looking dry. Whisk in 3 ounces sugar, a spoonful at a time, keeping the mixture always stiff. Fold in remaining sugar. Add a few drops of cochineal if liked to all or some of the meringue. Put the mixture into a piping bag with a large star nozzle and pipe stars on baking sheets, greased and lined with greased greaseproof paper or with waxed paper.

Dry meringues for 3 hours in lower part of oven set at Gas ¼/225°F., then turn off oven and leave to dry overnight. Whip the cream and colour pale pink if the meringues are white. Use to sandwich 2 stars together, by spooning on a blob or by piping some on half the stars. Arrange in little cake cases to serve.

Makes 10

Palmiers

13-ounce packet frozen puff
    pastry
1 large egg (beaten)
4 ounces caster sugar
5-ounce carton double cream
    (whipped)

ALLOW THE PASTRY to thaw at room temperature for at least 1 hour. Roll pastry to a 16-inch square, trimming the borders to make a perfect shape. Brush lightly with egg, sprinkle with caster sugar and fold sides of pastry to the centre. Brush with egg and sprinkle with sugar again and fold sides to the centre once more. Brush with egg, add sugar, fold one side on top of the other and press lightly. Brush with egg and sprinkle with sugar again on both sides. Cut the pastry roll into ½-inch slices using a sharp knife. Place on wet baking sheets, cut sides down, shaping the pastries by hand where the knife has flattened them slightly.

Bake for 10 minutes or until golden brown at Gas 7/425°F., then turn pastries and cook for 10–15 minutes more or until crisp. Cool on wire racks. Put the cream in a piping bag and pipe on half the palmiers. Sandwich with the remainder and serve at once. Store unfilled in an airtight tin if you want to keep the pastries.
Makes 10

Madeleines

4 ounces self-raising flour
pinch salt
4 ounces margarine
4 ounces caster sugar
2 large eggs
2 level tablespoons raspberry
 jam
2 ounces desiccated coconut
5 glacé cherries
angelica

SIFT THE FLOUR and salt. Cream the margarine and sugar and beat in the eggs one at a time. Fold in the flour. Half-fill 10 greased dariole moulds. Cook for 15–20 minutes at Gas 5/375°F. Turn out and cool on a wire rack.

Heat jam and brush all over the cakes. Roll each cake in coconut to cover completely. Allow jam to set. Decorate top of each with half a glacé cherry and a piece of angelica.
Makes 10

Brandy Snaps

2 ounces granulated sugar
2 level tablespoons golden
 syrup
2 ounces butter
2 ounces plain flour
pinch salt
1½ level teaspoons ground
 ginger
1 tablespoon lemon juice
 (strained)
5-ounce carton double cream
 (whipped)
1 tablespoon brandy

HEAT THE SUGAR, syrup and butter until melted. Sift the flour, salt and ginger and stir into the melted ingredients. Add the lemon juice and mix with a wooden spoon. Drop teaspoons of the mixture 4 inches apart on greased baking sheets. Cook for 10 minutes or until dark, golden brown at Gas 4/350°F. Leave to cool slightly on the sheets then slide off and roll round a wooden spoon handle. Leave to cool completely on wire racks.

Should any become too crisp to roll, return the baking sheet to the oven until the snaps soften again. Stir the cream and brandy together and put into a piping bag. Pipe cream into both ends of each snap and serve at once. If you want to store them, store unfilled in an airtight tin.

Should any break, crush them into fairly small pieces and use to sprinkle over ice-cream sweets.
Makes 10

Cardamom Cream Cookies

4 ounces butter
6 ounces caster sugar
1 large egg (beaten)
10 ounces plain flour
½ level teaspoon bicarbonate
of soda
½ level teaspoon baking
powder
pinch salt
1 level teaspoon ground
cardamom
5-ounce carton soured cream
vanilla sugar

CREAM THE BUTTER until light in colour and fluffy. Beat in the sugar and egg. Sift the flour, bicarbonate of soda, baking powder, salt and cardamom and stir alternately into the creamed mixture with the soured cream, ending with flour. Put the dough in the fridge overnight to rest.

Roll dough on a lightly floured board to ¼-inch thickness and cut into rounds using a 2½-inch fluted cutter. Place on ungreased baking sheets. Bake for about 12 minutes at Gas 5/375°F. Turn on to a wire rack to cool and sprinkle with vanilla sugar.
Makes 30

Danish Pastries

½ ounce dried yeast
10 tablespoons tepid water
1 pound plain flour
11 ounces unsalted butter
1 ounce caster sugar
½ level teaspoon ground
cardamom
½ level teaspoon salt
2 large eggs (beaten)

SPRINKLE THE YEAST on the tepid water and leave it in a warm place for 15 minutes or until it is frothy on top. Sift the flour into a bowl. Rub in 2 ounces butter. Stir in the sugar, spice and salt. Make a well in the centre; pour in the yeast liquid and the eggs. Mix to an elastic dough. Turn on to a floured board and knead for 3 minutes until smooth and pliable. Cover dough and allow to rise in a warm place until doubled in size.

Work remaining butter with a palette knife until soft then shape it into a square block. Roll pastry to a 12-inch oblong, put butter in centre and quickly pat it over entire surface using your fingertips. Fold in three and chill in the fridge for 30 minutes. Roll again to an oblong about ½-inch thick and fold and chill again. Repeat this process twice more then roll to ½-inch thickness, fold pastry in half and chill for at least 30 minutes before using. Shape and finish as follows, using the following ingredients as indicated under each heading.

2 ounces bought marzipan
1 large egg (beaten)
glacé icing (see page 46)
confectioners' custard
(see page 46)
½ ounce almond nibs

1 ounce butter
1 ounce caster sugar
1 level teaspoon ground
cinnamon
1 ounce sultanas
1 ounce chopped mixed peel

Crescent

Roll a quarter of the dough to a 10-inch square. Cut into 4 squares then cut each square into 2 triangles. Put a small piece of marzipan in the middle of the longest side of each triangle. Roll from this side to the point, curving the roll round to make a crescent. Arrange on baking sheets and leave for about 20 minutes in a warm place until puffy. Brush with beaten egg and bake for about 10 minutes or until golden brown at Gas 7/425°F. Brush with glacé icing while still warm, and cool.

Triangles
Roll a quarter of the dough to a 10-inch square and then cut into 4 smaller squares. Put 1 teaspoon confectioners' custard in the centre of each square and fold in half to form triangles. Press edges well to seal in the filling. Place on a baking sheet. Allow to rise for about 20 minutes then brush with egg and sprinkle with the chopped nuts. Bake for 10 minutes at Gas 7/425°F. Spoon a little glacé icing on each while still warm.

Pinwheels
Roll a quarter of the dough to an oblong 12 inches by 8 inches. Beat the butter, sugar and cinnamon until smooth and soft and spread over the dough. Scatter with the sultanas and mixed peel. Roll from one short end to form a thick roll. Cut into 1-inch slices and arrange cut side down on greased baking sheets. Flatten slightly then leave in a warm place for 20 minutes to rise. Bake for about 10 minutes at Gas 7/425°F. Spread with glacé icing while warm and leave to cool.

Cushions
Roll remaining pastry to a 10-inch square and cut into 4 smaller squares. Put 1 level teaspoon confectioners' custard in the centre of each square and pinch the corners in the centre to seal. Allow to rise for 20 minutes as before then brush with egg and bake for 10 minutes at Gas 7/425°F. Brush with glacé icing while warm and allow to cool.
Makes 24

Almond Biscuits

8 ounces butter
8 ounces caster sugar
5 ounces plain flour
2 ounces almond nibs

CREAM THE BUTTER and sugar together until light and fluffy. Sift the flour and stir it into the creamed mixture with the almonds. Work the dough with your hands until smooth, then form it into 2 rolls each about 2 inches in diameter. Wrap in greaseproof paper and chill in the fridge for 8 hours or overnight.

Next day, slice the rolls thinly. Arrange the biscuits on greased baking sheets and bake for about 10 minutes at Gas 4/350°F. Cool on racks.
Makes 36

Iced Coffee

1 pint strong black coffee
2–4 ounces caster sugar
1 pint cold milk
½ pint single cream

MAKE THE COFFEE very strong and black and sweeten to taste with 2–4 ounces of sugar, bearing in mind that the coffee will be diluted by the milk and cream. Stir in the milk and leave to chill in the fridge for at least 4 hours. Just before serving, stir in the cream and pour into glasses. Serve with straws.
Serves 8

Drop Scones

8 ounces plain flour
pinch salt
2 ounces caster sugar
½ pint buttermilk
1 level teaspoon bicarbonate
  of soda
2 ounces lard

SIFT THE FLOUR and salt. Make a well in the centre and add the sugar and all but 1 tablespoon of the buttermilk. Mix to a stiff smooth batter. Dissolve the bicarbonate of soda in the remaining buttermilk and stir it into the batter. Beat well.

Grease a girdle or very heavy frying-pan with a little of the lard. When hot drop tablespoons of the batter on to the surface forming each one into a round with the tip of the spoon. Cook for about 2 minutes or until golden underneath, then flip them over and cook for about 1 minute more. Serve with honeypot spread.
Makes 12

Honeypot Spread

6 heaped tablespoons honey
1 tablespoon lemon juice
  (strained)
1 level teaspoon ground
  cinnamon
1 ounce sultanas
1 ounce walnuts (chopped)

PUT THE HONEY, lemon juice, spice and sultanas in a pan. Heat gently, stirring until the honey becomes runny. Stir in the nuts and turn into a pot to serve.
Serves 6

4

Supper Parties

SUPPER HAS MANY different meanings throughout the country—'posh' in London and the south and really meaning dinner; homely in the north meaning, to my family at any rate, the biscuits and cocoa prepared just before going to bed. I like to think of supper parties as those that are homely and involve really close friends ... the meal you'd make after a game of cards or the meal you'd make for a dear friend who'd dropped in unexpectedly. Into this category come dishes like pasties, steak and kidney puddings and pies, Welsh rarebit or buck rarebit with a poached egg on top, toasted sandwiches and sausages and mash. I don't think there's a single rule of entertaining that can't be broken for a supper party. Make it as informal as you like—formal ones belong to the Jane Austen books. Sit people on the floor with their plates and forks or let them perch with them on their knees. Serve beer or wine, tea or coffee, or whatever people fancy. Rustle up a pud using store-cupboard ingredients to save time: dumplings with a syrup sauce are very quick. If you have more time, make a bread and butter pudding, or a steamed jam pudding.

This kind of supper party is ideal if you're living in a bedsitter. Space is usually short and the space to cook and the time in which to do it are usually shorter. Landladies assume that people who live in bedsits have midget appetites and are masters of cooking, whereas the opposite is usually the case. If the bedsit occupant is away from home and mother's cooking for the first time, he or she may have difficulty in boiling an egg, let alone thinking out a hundred and one different and nutritious ways of preparing a meal on one ring in a cupboard. Here are some ways to get round this problem.

Pancakes can be made in advance and layered between sheets of foil. They can be filled, rolled, arranged in a dish and covered with a sauce to be baked in the oven later for a savoury or sweet dish which looks impressive to a guest. If you're literally stuck with no oven, a stew (but special) is the answer. Beef stroganoff or Portuguese veal are both delicious and cook quickly. Serve either with rice or noodles or other pasta shapes.

Make starters which require no cooking, such as marinated kippers—which taste and look something like smoked salmon, especially if started a couple of days in advance; or melon with *prosciutto*—the very thinly-sliced raw ham, of which Parma is the best known—which is filling and delicious; alternatively, *crudités* served with a garlicky mayonnaise dressing make a cheap and cheerful first course. For a main course try risotto—mainly rice, with a few mushrooms, shrimps, peas or other inexpensive ingredients mixed in. This is the kind of dish that expands or contracts according to the size of one's purse at the time of the supper party. It's good with grated cheese added and heated gently until it goes sticky. Lasagne layered with a meaty sauce (less meat and more tomato as the week goes on) and covered with a well-flavoured white or cheese sauce makes a substantial main course, too.

There are lots of ways in which you can trim the cost of entertaining, but if you want to make a little look marvellous spend some time on the garnish. Gherkin fans, cucumber cones, lemon butterflies, spring onion flowers, radish roses, all take time but little money and look fantastic. Add them to your savoury courses. Sweet dishes will benefit from a sprinkling of caster or icing sugar, grated chocolate if cold, and raisins or sultanas (plumped with 1 tablespoon real rum, sherry or other spirit), can perk up a plain pud such as vanilla ice cream or a bought mousse.

Garnishes and decorations

Lemon butterflies   Cut a lemon into thin slices, then cut each slice in half. Cut almost into quarters but leave joined at the centre pithy bit. Open out into 2 butterfly wings.

Lemon twists   Cut a lemon into slices, then cut through to the centre of each slice. Holding the peel on either side of the cut, twist the slice in opposite directions, one piece towards you, one away, and arrange the resulting twist on your dish.

Lemon flowers   Using a small sharp knife, cut through to the middle of the lemon at its fattest part with the knife on a slant. Remove the knife, slant it the opposite way to complete the V and cut through to the centre. Continue in this way round the lemon, making sure that the cuts are all equal in depth, go through to the centre and are going to meet. Gently pull the two halves apart. Cut a slice off each lemon half at the base so that it will stand flat. The same can be done with tomatoes and oranges.

Lemon wedges   These should be cut across the fruit and not from the calyx to stalk end.

Radish roses   Using a sharp knife cut the radish almost in half from the root end. Don't cut all the way through or it will fall to pieces. Holding the halves together, cut into quarters and then into eighths. Drop into iced water for about 1 hour or until the petals open out. If you're very handy with your knife, cut into eighths but only through the skin, then peel each segment of skin down almost to the stalk. If liked you can continue to do this with the white inside. Again drop into cold water until the petals open out.

Spring onion flowers   Trim off the roots and cut the onions into 2-inch lengths. Cut from the green part almost to the root end cutting the onion into quarters or eighths if you've got a steady hand. Put in iced water until the leaves open out.

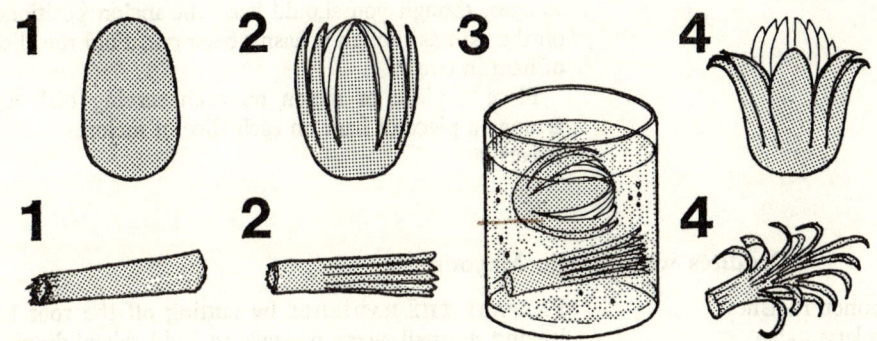

Gherkin fans   You need a sharp knife and a fairly flat gherkin. Cut downwards from the pointed end to the blunt end in fairly thin slices leaving about $\frac{1}{4}$-inch intact at the bottom. Spread the slices into a fan shape.

Cucumber cones   Cut thin slices of cucumber, preferably unpeeled. Cut each slice to the centre and wrap round to form a cone. Secure with cocktail sticks and then arrange with the cut sides down to hold them firm. Cucumber cones can be piped with savoury butters (see page 25) if liked.

Celery curls   Cut a celery stalk into strips about $\frac{1}{2}$ inch wide and 2 inches long. Cut along the length almost to the end but leave about $\frac{1}{4}$ inch joined at the bottom. Drop into iced water for 2 hours to allow the fringed end to curl.

Crimped cucumber   Run a fork down the sides of an unpeeled cucumber to remove some of the peel, then cut into slices.

Citrus fruit strips   You need a canelle knife for this. Holding an orange, lemon or grapefruit in your left hand, bring the knife towards you. By pressing the knife, it will cut a thin thread of peel which is perfect for decorating drinks, puddings, pies and desserts.

Chocolate cones   Make tiny greaseproof paper bags like icing bags and fill the point up to 1 inch with melted chocolate. Leave to set. Or drop just a little chocolate into the bag and let it run round the paper to coat it, or you can use a paint brush to brush the paper to coat it. Give the paper a second or even third coat to make these hollow cones fairly sturdy. Leave to set then carefully peel off the paper.

Chocolate leaves   Use well-washed rose leaves and drag each one across the surface of melted chocolate. Leave to set then carefully peel off the leaf, leaving a chocolate replica.

Parma Ham with Melon

1 small Honeydew melon
4 slices Parma ham

CUT THE MELON into 4 slices. Cut the melon from the skin and slice down to the skin to make bite-sized wedges, though you should keep the melon positioned on the skin as though it hasn't been cut. Fold the slices of ham in two.

Place a piece of melon on each serving dish and arrange a piece of ham on each slice of melon.
Serves 4

Crudités with Garlic Mayonnaise

1 bunch radishes
8 celery stalks
6 good carrots
8 spring onions
½ small cauliflower
1 green pepper
mayonnaise (see page 19)
4 garlic cloves (crushed)

PREPARE THE RADISHES by cutting off the root but leaving a small piece of stalk to hold when dipping. Scrub the celery stalks and cut into 3-inch lengths. Remove the roots and damaged parts from the carrots, and scrape or peel. Cut lengthways into 3-inch lengths, about as thick as the spring onions. Top and tail the onions and cut into 3-inch lengths. Separate the cauliflower into florets. Remove the core and seeds from the pepper and cut the flesh into strips. Arrange all the vegetables on a large round plate leaving room for a small dish in the centre. Mix the mayonnaise with the garlic and spoon into the centre dish.
Serves 8

Pineapple Upside-Down Pudding

6 ounces butter
2 ounces Demerara sugar
12-ounce can pineapple rings
4 ounces caster sugar
2 large eggs (beaten)
6 ounces self-raising flour
1 level teaspoon arrowroot

CREAM 2 OUNCES butter with the Demerara sugar and spread over the base of a 7-inch round cake tin or soufflé dish. Drain the pineapple rings and arrange the fruit in the base of the tin or dish. Cream the remaining butter and caster sugar until fluffy. Beat in the eggs, then fold in the flour and mix to a soft dropping consistency with a little pineapple juice. Spread this mixture carefully over the fruit. Bake for about 45 minutes at Gas 4/350°F.

While it cooks, blend the arrowroot with 4 tablespoons cold water. Bring the remaining pineapple juice to the boil. Pour on to the arrowroot, stir well and return to the pan. Bring to boil and cook gently for 3 minutes, stirring all the time the sauce thickens and clears. When the pudding is cooked, turn it on to a serving dish so that the pineapple is on top and serve with the sauce.
Serves 6

Bread and Butter Pudding

8 thin slices white bread
3 ounces butter
3 ounces sultanas
2 ounces Demerara sugar
1 level teaspoon ground
  cinnamon
1 level tablespoon caster sugar
2 large eggs
¾ pint milk

CUT THE CRUSTS off the bread and spread the slices with the butter. Cut 4 slices in half diagonally, the remainder into 1-inch wide fingers. Arrange the triangles around the edge of an oval ovenproof dish, points upwards. Cover the base of the dish with half the fingers. Sprinkle with half the sultanas and half the Demerara sugar and the cinnamon. Cover with the remaining bread fingers and sprinkle with remaining sultanas. Put the caster sugar, eggs and milk in a basin and whisk well until mixed. Pour over the bread and butter pudding and sprinkle with the remaining Demerara sugar. Bake for 1 hour at Gas 5/375°F. Serve hot or cold with custard.

Serves 6

Steak and Kidney Pie

1 large onion (chopped)
2 ounces dripping
1 pound chuck steak
½ pound ox kidney
1 beef stock cube
1 pint boiling water
salt and pepper
12 ounces plain flour
3 ounces lard
3 ounces margarine

COOK THE ONION in the dripping for 5 minutes. Cut the steak into 1-inch cubes. Remove skin and core from the kidney and cut into ½-inch pieces. Add the beef and kidney to the pan and cook for 5 minutes until golden brown on all sides. Transfer the meat and onion to an oval ovenproof dish. Dissolve the stock cube in the boiling water and add it to the dish with salt and pepper to taste. Cover the dish with a lid or foil and cook for 1½ hours at Gas 3/325°F.

Sift the flour with a pinch of salt. Rub in the lard and margarine and mix to a stiff dough with cold water. Lightly flour a working surface and roll the dough until it is 1 inch bigger all round than the pie dish. Allow the pie to cool a little, then cut off a ½-inch strip all round the pastry and press it round the rim of the dish, which should be greased. Moisten this strip and cover with the large piece of pastry. Trim the edge and decorate. Make a hole in the centre to let the steam escape. Cook for 20–25 minutes at Gas 7/425°F. Serve hot.

Serves 4–6

Steak Pudding

1 pound skirt steak
seasoned flour
8 ounces self-raising flour
salt and pepper
4 ounces shredded suet
4 ounces mushrooms (sliced)
1 large onion (chopped)
1 beef stock cube
¼ pint boiling water

CUT THE STEWING steak into 1-inch pieces. Toss the meat in seasoned flour. Sift the self-raising flour with a pinch of salt. Stir in the suet and mix to a soft but not sticky dough with cold water. Roll the dough on a lightly floured board to a ¼-inch thick round big enough to fit a 2-pint pudding basin. Cut out a quarter triangle for the lid. Line a greased basin with the large piece, moisten the cut edges and press well to seal. Fill the basin alternately with meat, mushrooms and onions. Dissolve the stock cube in the boiling water. Season the meat and pour on the stock. Roll the remaining piece of pastry to a circle just large enough for the top of the basin. Moisten the edges of pastry and press well to seal. Cover the basin loosely with foil and steam pudding for 4 hours, replacing the water in the pan with boiling water as it boils away.
Serves 6

Dumpling Dessert

8 ounces self-raising flour
1 level teaspoon salt
water
4 level tablespoons golden syrup
2 tablespoons lemon juice (strained)

SIFT THE FLOUR and salt into a bowl. Mix with about ¼ pint and 4 tablespoons cold water to make a dough. Form into about 8 balls, flouring your hands each time. Steam for about 20 minutes but do not remove the steamer lid during the cooking time or the dumplings become sad in the middle.

Heat the golden syrup with the lemon juice until hot and runny. Serve the dumplings with the lemony syrup poured over.
Serves 4

Ice Cream with Rum and Raisin Sauce

1 family block vanilla ice cream
4 ounces seedless raisins
1 tablespoon rum
2 ounces Demerara sugar
½ pint cold water
1 ounce walnuts (roughly chopped)

CUT THE BLOCK of ice cream into 6 portions but leave in the ice-making compartment until the actual moment of serving. Put the raisins in a basin and add the rum. Leave to soak for 10 minutes. Dissolve the sugar in the water over a gentle heat, then bring to the boil and boil rapidly for 5 minutes. Stir in the raisins and rum. Cool slightly. Pour quickly over the ice cream, sprinkle with the walnuts and serve at once. Or you might like to serve the sauce in a small jug.
Serves 6

Poor Knights of Windsor

12 ½-inch thick slices of
   white bread
½ pint milk
3 ounces caster sugar
1 large egg
4 ounces butter
6 ounces strawberry jam

CUT THE CRUSTS off the bread. Whisk the milk, sugar and egg together on a flat plate. Quickly dip in the bread slices on both sides to moisten. Don't let them become soggy. Fry in butter until crisp on both sides and golden brown. Quickly spread with jam, cut into fingers if liked and serve at once.
Serves 6

Sausages and Mash

8 large sausages
1½ pounds potatoes (peeled)
2 large onions (chopped)
½ pint cold water
2 beef stock cubes
½ pint boiling water
1 level tablespoon cornflour
salt and pepper

DIVIDE THE SAUSAGES and fry very gently at first until the fat runs, then continue cooking, turning frequently, for about 20 minutes or until the sausages are well cooked. Cook the potatoes in boiling salted water for about 20 minutes or until soft enough to mash. While the sausages and mash cook, boil the onion in the cold water, until soft and cooked. Dissolve the stock cubes in the boiling water. Blend the cornflour with a little cold water and gradually pour on the hot stock. Pour this mixture into the onions and bring to the boil, stirring all the time while the mixture thickens and then cook gently for 5 minutes. Season with salt and pepper. Drain the sausages. Mash the potatoes with plenty of salt and pepper and pile the mash on a serving dish. Arrange the sausages around the mash and serve the onion gravy separately.
Serves 4

Triple Decker Toasty

4 rashers streaky bacon
8 ounces mushrooms (sliced)
2 ounces butter
4 large eggs (beaten)
salt and pepper
16 slices white bread
6 tomatoes (quartered)

REMOVE THE BACON rinds and cut the rashers into small pieces. Fry the rinds until the fat runs, then add the rashers and cook gently until tender but not crisp. Meanwhile cook the mushrooms in 1 ounce butter in a small saucepan for about 5 minutes. Scramble the eggs with salt and pepper in the remaining butter.

While the fillings cook, toast the bread and keep it hot. Cover 4 slices toast with well-drained bacon pieces. Top with a second slice and cover each one with mushrooms. Top with another slice of toast and scrambled egg. Finally add the last slice and garnish each toasty with tomato quarters.
Serves 4

Welsh Rarebit

6 tablespoons brown ale
10 ounces Cheddar cheese
  (grated)
salt and pepper
1 level teaspoon made
  mustard
2 ounces butter
6 slices white bread

POUR THE ALE into a pan with the cheese and melt the cheese slowly. Season with salt, pepper and mustard, then stir in the butter. Toast the bread on both sides. Spread the mixture over each slice and return to the grill to brown on top.
Serves 6

Buck Rarebit

Welsh Rarebit mixture (see
  above)
6 slices white bread
6 large eggs
little vinegar

MAKE THE WELSH rarebit mixture and put to one side. Toast the bread. Poach the eggs in water to which 1 tablespoon vinegar has been added for flavour. Drain the eggs well. Cover the toast with the cheese mixture, brown under the grill, then top with a poached egg.
Serves 6

Portuguese Veal

1 pound shoulder of veal
½ ounce lard
¼ pint dry white wine
2 level teaspoons ground
  cumin
1 garlic clove (crushed)
salt and pepper
3 thin slices lemon
1 level teaspoon ground
  coriander

CUT THE MEAT into 1-inch cubes and pat dry with kitchen paper. Heat the lard in a frying-pan; fry the veal to brown on all sides, turning it frequently. Stir in all but 2 tablespoons of the wine, the cumin, garlic, a good pinch each of salt and pepper, preferably freshly ground black pepper. Bring to the boil and cook for about 40 minutes or until tender. Add the remaining wine. Cut the lemon slices into quarters, stir into the veal. Cook stirring for 5 minutes more, then stir in the coriander and serve at once.
Serves 4

Beef Stroganoff

1½ pounds rump steak
1 ounce butter
1 large onion (chopped)
8 ounces button mushrooms
  (sliced)
salt and pepper
½ ounce plain flour
1 beef stock cube
¼ pint boiling water
5-ounce carton soured cream
parsley (finely chopped)

CUT THE STEAK into strips each 2 inches long and ½ inch wide. Melt the butter and fry the onion for 5 minutes, stirring. Add the steak and cook for 5 minutes more. Add the mushrooms and season with salt and pepper. Continue cooking for 5 minutes more or until meat is tender. Sprinkle on the flour and mix well.

Dissolve the stock cube in the boiling water and stir into the pan a little at a time. Bring to the boil, stirring while the stroganoff becomes thicker. Cook for about 5 minutes, then lower the heat and stir in the cream. Do not boil the mixture once you've added the cream. Serve with rice, sprinkling the meat with the parsley.
Serves 4–6

Spinach Pancakes

2 11-ounce packets frozen
  spinach
1 large onion (chopped)
1 garlic clove (crushed)
2 tablespoons cooking oil
8 ounces lean raw minced
  meat
salt and pepper
4 ounces plain flour
1 large egg
1 pint milk
lard
½-pint packet cheese sauce mix
2 ounces Cheddar cheese (grated)

COOK THE SPINACH according to packet instructions. Cook the onion, garlic, oil and mince together for about 15 minutes or until the mince is cooked. Season with salt and pepper. While it cooks, make the pancakes. Sift the flour with a pinch of salt. Make a well in the centre, drop in the egg and mix to a smooth batter with ½ pint milk. Cook 8 pancakes using a little lard to grease the frying-pan each time. Fill each pancake with a little meat mixture and some spinach, roll up and arrange in a heatproof dish. Make up the cheese sauce using the remaining milk and pour it over the pancakes. Sprinkle with the cheese and brown under a hot grill. *Serves 4*

Risotto

1 large onion (chopped)
4 ounces mushrooms
  (chopped)
4 tablespoons cooking oil
8 ounces Patna rice
1 large chicken joint (cooked)
2 ounces ham (cooked)
2 chicken stock cubes
1½ pints boiling water
salt and pepper
4 hard-boiled eggs

COOK THE ONION and mushrooms in the oil for 5 minutes. Stir in the rice and cook for 2 minutes more, stirring frequently. Cut the chicken and ham into bite-sized pieces. Dissolve the stock cubes in the boiling water and pour over the rice. Bring to the boil, then reduce the heat and simmer until almost all of the stock has been absorbed by the rice. Stir in the chicken and ham and season with salt and pepper. Cut the eggs into quarters and stir through the risotto at the last moment. Heat through and serve at once. *Serves 4*

Lasagne

1 large onion (chopped)
1 garlic clove (chopped)
1 stick celery (chopped)
2 tablespoons cooking oil
8 ounces raw minced meat
½ ounce cornflour
1 level teaspoon dried thyme
salt and pepper
15-ounce can tomatoes
4 level tablespoons tomato
  purée
½ ounce butter
½ ounce plain flour
½ pint milk
3 ounces Cheddar cheese
  (grated)
6 ounces lasagne

COOK THE ONION, garlic and celery in the oil for 5 minutes. Stir in the meat and cook for about 5 minutes or until well browned. Stir in the cornflour, thyme and salt and pepper, tomatoes and their juice and the tomato purée. Bring to the boil and simmer for 15 minutes.

Meanwhile, melt the butter in a pan, stir in the flour to make a roux, then stir in the milk off the heat. Bring to the boil, stirring all the time and cook for 3 minutes. Stir in 2 ounces cheese. Cook the lasagne in plenty of boiling salted water for about 10 minutes. Drain well. Layer the lasagne, meat and cheese sauces in a deep ovenproof dish, beginning with the pasta and ending with the cheese sauce. Sprinkle with the remaining cheese and bake for about 40 minutes at Gas 5/375°F. *Serves 4*

Marinated Kippers

2 7-ounce packets frozen
  kipper fillets
1 large onion (sliced)
freshly ground black pepper
juice of 3 lemons (strained)
vegetable oil
parsley (finely chopped)

ALLOW THE KIPPERS to thaw at room temperature, then remove the skin from each fillet using a sharp knife. Separate the onion slices into rings. Arrange the kippers in a flat serving dish and sprinkle with the onion rings. Sprinkle well with black pepper and pour on the lemon juice and oil to just cover. Leave, covered, in the fridge for 2-3 days.

To serve sprinkle with parsley, and provide thin brown bread and butter separately.

Serves 6

Chicken Pasties

2 chicken joints (cooked)
4 ounces ham (cooked)
12 ounces plain flour
salt and pepper
3 ounces lard
3 ounces margarine
2 heaped tablespoons
  mayonnaise (see page 19)
oil or fat for deep frying
watercress sprigs

REMOVE THE SKIN from the chicken joints and cut the chicken into small pieces. Chop the ham. Sift the flour with a pinch of salt. Rub in the lard and margarine and mix to a stiff dough with cold water. Roll out on a lightly floured board and cut out 4-inch rounds using a plain cutter. Mix the mayonnaise into the chicken and ham and season with salt and pepper. Use to fill the pastry rounds. Moisten the edges with cold water, fold over to make the pasties, and press the edges well to seal.

Fry for about 4 minutes or until flaky-looking and golden brown. Garnish with watercress.

Serves 8

5

Barbecues

THE BIG ADVANTAGE of barbecues, for both guest and host, is that the guests do a lot of the work. Even the man who won't set foot in the kitchen at home seems to delight in looking after a charcoal fire outdoors. It's necessary to provide plenty of large aprons for those who are going to take an active part and also plenty of long-handled implements. Paper plates and napkins should be provided in large numbers. Most food will have been planned to be eaten with the fingers or simply wrapped in a napkin, so keep piles of them around for mopping-up operations. Glasses, like napkins, tend to be used once only for outdoor parties—more places for them to be put down and lost. So provide two per guest of the sturdy kitchen tumbler type rather than anything fragile and certainly not anything expensive or precious.

Plan food which can either be eaten with the fingers or with plastic cutlery—which doesn't need washing up afterwards. It's a pest hunting for missing items from your best canteen. Food shouldn't be too fine for a barbecue party. People really prefer good chunky sizes like whole cutlets, chicken drumsticks, good thick hamburgers, and great wedges of hot French bread.

Drinks should be kept simple too. A keg of beer from which guests help themselves seems the simplest solution and one of the cheapest. Wine is good too, but it needs to be one of the more robust plonky sort rather than something which requires more attention than it is likely to receive at a barbecue. Italian reds go well with this kind of food.

Puddings may be provided but again the kind that can be eaten with the fingers seem to be the most successful, although at this stage of the party people will probably be sitting in groups rather than standing about round the barbecue itself. You may feel inclined, therefore, to provide something which requires a spoon (like the winter fruit salad).

Lighting a barbecue party requires a certain amount of ingenuity. For those of us with small gardens, the lights from the house will probably be quite adequate. If you want to light corners for the effect, use candles stuck in the earth, surrounded by glass lampshades (cut-down bottles—see page 90), or use small oil lamps

Fun for a children's party are Ring Doughnuts (page 85), Cheese Straws (page 85), Jelly Slices (page 86) and Lemonade (page 83). Make a Hansel and Gretel Cottage (page 86) and cover it with lots of sweets

(which Woolworth stores sell in case of gas or power cuts). Candles stuck in jam jars can also light the garden but need fixing to the glass with melted wax so they don't fall over and blow out.

Make sure you have plenty of garden seats or old blankets and cushions handy, otherwise people will tend to grab what's nearest: you'll find your party spirit getting strained if you spot your best cushion on the damp grass.

While it's marvellous to go out and buy a barbecue, one with all the implements to match and possibly with a spit as well, it's perfectly possible to build your own. You'll need lots of bricks—at least twenty, a shelf from the oven and an old baking tin to hold the charcoal. First, make two lines of bricks, which should be close enough to stand the oven shelf on top to form the grid. Add more bricks to make a square. Stand the rim of the baking tin on these bricks. You may have to adjust them, but the idea is to keep the tin off the grass and then you won't have a burnt patch. Add more bricks to the walls of the barbecue to keep the tin in place and also to make sure the grid is well above the charcoal. Put the oven shelf on top. Fill the tin with charcoal and that's your barbecue. It has the advantage that it won't come to harm if left in the rain and it's easily dismantled when the barbecue is over.

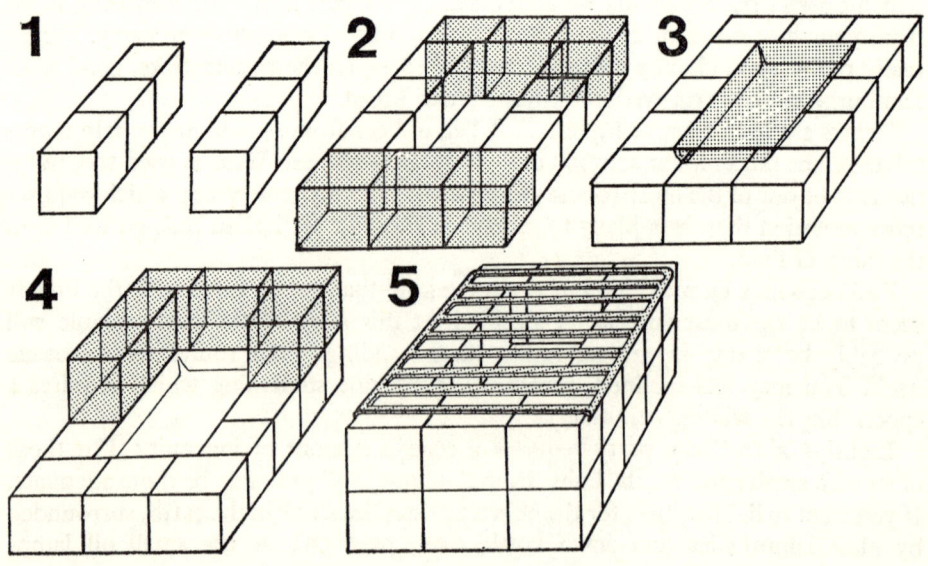

Danish Open Sandwiches
(page 94)

Charcoal can be bought at most hardware stores nowadays, or in the garden section of department stores, as well as at coal offices. Ask when you're buying it for a quick lighting fluid for charcoal. If you can't find any, light the charcoal with firelighters and paper and allow 1 hour for the charcoal to become red hot all over the surface. Don't, please, use methylated spirits or petrol. It's far too risky. Charcoal doesn't really work if you add to it. It's far better to get a lot going in the first place. It will keep hot enough to cook everything. Once you add to charcoal, it reduces the heat and it takes another hour to become red hot again.

Corn on the Cob in Foil

8 whole sweetcorn cobs
salt and pepper
2 ounces butter

STRIP EACH CORN cob of its leaves and silky white threads. Put each cob in a piece of foil large enough to wrap round it. Season with salt and pepper, and add a knob of butter. Fold over the foil and twist the ends to seal. Put on the barbecue grid and leave for about 10 minutes, depending on how hot the coals are. Turn back the foil to eat and use it to prevent burnt fingers.

Serves 8

Spit-Roasted Chicken

3-pound chicken
salt and pepper
2 garlic cloves (skinned)
1 level teaspoon dried
   marjoram

Barbecue sauce:
2 large onions (chopped)
1 ounce butter
½ pint tomato ketchup
¼ pint pineapple juice
salt and pepper

WIPE THE CHICKEN inside and out and season with salt and pepper. Fry the onions in the butter until golden and soft, then stir in the ketchup and pineapple juice, season to taste and simmer for 20 minutes. While it simmers, push the garlic and herbs into the cavity of the chicken and arrange on the spit of your barbecue. Brush with the barbecue sauce and cook for about 2 hours, basting often with the sauce. When cooked, the drumsticks will move quite easily and no pink juices will run if you push a sharp knife into the thickest part of the flesh. Cooking times will vary enormously, depending on how hot your charcoal is and how near to the heat your spit is.

Serves 8–12

Cheeseburgers

1 small onion (chopped)
1 small egg (beaten)
¾ pound raw minced beef
salt and pepper
1 garlic clove (crushed)
2 ounces lard
4 square slices processed
  cheese
4 soft rolls (toasted)
pickle

MIX THE ONION and egg into the beef and season with
the salt and pepper and garlic. Form into 4 flat cakes and
fry in the lard for about 10 minutes, turning occasionally.
Put one hamburger with a slice of cheese between the
halves of each roll (toasted on the cut side only). Serve
garnished with a spoonful of brown pickle.
Serves 4

American Burgers

1 large onion (chopped)
1 large egg (beaten)
1½ pounds raw minced beef
salt and pepper
4 ounces dripping
2 large tomatoes (sliced)
4 lettuce leaves (washed)
8 slices cucumber
2 heaped tablespoons salad
  cream
4 large soft rolls

MIX THE ONION and egg into the minced beef with
plenty of salt and pepper to season. Form the mixture
into 8 flat cakes and fry in dripping for about 10 minutes,
turning the hamburgers from time to time. Drain well.
Put two hamburgers with tomato slices, lettuce, cucumber and salad cream into each soft roll. Serve wrapped
in paper napkins.
Serves 4

Hot Diggety Dogs

8 soft long rolls
8 level teaspoons made
  mustard
8 frankfurter sausages
2 large onions (chopped)
1 tablespoon vegetable oil
1 level teaspoon chilli powder

CUT THE ROLLS lengthways almost in half. Spread each
roll with 1 level teaspoon of mustard. Cook the frankfurter sausages according to the directions on the can,
or if not the canned variety drop into boiling water and
simmer for about 5 minutes until heated through.
Meanwhile fry the onion in the oil for about 10 minutes
or until soft and cooked. Sprinkle with the chilli
powder, stir well and spread on each roll. Drain the
frankfurters, add one to each roll and serve wrapped in a
paper napkin.
Serves 8

Barbecued Herrings

6 herrings
2 ounces margarine
1 large onion (chopped)
4 ounces fresh white breadcrumbs
1 level teaspoon dried thyme

ASK YOUR FISHMONGER to gut each herring but to
leave the head and tail on. Melt the margarine and fry
the onion for about 10 minutes or until soft and golden
brown. Stir in the breadcrumbs, thyme and parsley
and season well with salt and pepper. Use to stuff the
herrings. Wrap each herring in foil, seasoning the fish

1 level tablespoon parsley
  (finely chopped)
salt and pepper
2 ounces butter

with salt and pepper and adding a knob of butter. Grill on the barbecue for about 20 minutes or until tender.
Serves 6

Fruit Kebabs

1 eating apple
2 large bananas
juice of 1 lemon (strained)
16 strawberries
16 white grapes
16 black grapes
12-ounce can pineapple
  pieces
juice of 1 orange (strained)
2 ounces Demerara sugar

CORE THE APPLE and cut it into 16 chunks. Peel and thickly slice the bananas. Sprinkle with the lemon juice to prevent them browning. Thread the fruits on to 8 skewers. Mix the pineapple juice with the orange and lemon juice remaining from the apple and banana and stir in the sugar. Use to brush the fruit kebabs. Grill on the barbecue, brushing frequently, and serve when the fruit is soft on the outside but still crisp inside. Serve the juice separately.
Serves 8

Banana Rich

8 large bananas
24 marshmallows
8 ounces plain chocolate
1 level teaspoon ground
  nutmeg
2 ounces almond nibs
  (toasted)

PEEL THE BANANAS and arrange them in a large foil dish. Cut each marshmallow into pieces and sprinkle over the bananas. Roughly chop the chocolate and add to the dish. Sprinkle with the nutmeg. Cover with foil and put on the grid of the barbecue. Bake for about 25 minutes or until the bananas are tender and the chocolate has melted. Serve sprinkled with the almonds.
Serves 8

Polynesian Steaks

2 pounds rump steak
¼ pint tomato ketchup
few drops Worcester sauce
salt and pepper
8 pineapple rings

ASK THE BUTCHER to cut the piece of steak in one complete piece. Lay it flat on a hot barbecue to sear one side, then turn and sear the other side. Mix the tomato ketchup with a few drops of Worcester sauce and seasoning to taste and brush over the steak, cooking each side for about 5 minutes, or longer if you like steak well done.

While it cooks, barbecue the pineapple rings until soft and just becoming golden brown. Cut the steak into 8 pieces and top each piece with a pineapple ring to serve.
Serves 8

Bean and Onion Salad

20-ounce can haricot beans
1 small onion (chopped)
vinaigrette (see page 19)
1 level tablespoon parsley
  (chopped)

DRAIN THE BEANS of their water and rinse in plenty of fresh cold water. Mix with the onion and vinaigrette and sprinkle with parsley to serve.
Serves 8

Gingered Lamb Cutlets

8 lamb cutlets
6 tablespoons soy sauce
3 tablespoons vegetable oil
1 level teaspoon mustard
　powder
1 level teaspoon ground
　ginger
salt and pepper
2 garlic cloves (crushed)
pinch caster sugar
parsley (finely chopped)

PUT THE CUTLETS in a dish. Mix the soy sauce with the oil, mustard, ground ginger, salt and pepper, garlic, sugar and parsley and whisk well. Pour over the lamb and leave for 4 hours. Drain cutlets and arrange on the hot barbecue. Cook, basting frequently with the marinade for about 15 minutes or until tender.
Serves 8

Garlic Bread

1 French loaf
1 garlic clove (crushed)
6 ounces butter

CUT THE LOAF diagonally into 1½-inch chunks but do not cut right through each slice. Leave the loaf joined along the base. Beat the crushed garlic into the butter until it is really soft. Spread the butter on the bread slices inside the cuts. Wrap the whole loaf in foil and bake for about 10 minutes on the barbecue grid.
Serves 8

Winter Fruit Salad

6 ounces prunes
6 ounces dried apricots
4 ounces dried figs
4 ounces sultanas
4 ounces chopped mixed peel
1½ pints cold water
4 ounces soft brown sugar
juice of 1 lemon (strained)
6 whole cloves

PUT THE PRUNES, apricots, figs, sultanas and mixed peel in a large pan with the cold water. Stir in the sugar and bring slowly to the boil. Simmer for 30 minutes over a very gentle heat. Stir in the lemon juice and cloves and serve hot or cold.
Serves 6

Curry Dip

5-ounce carton soured cream
5 level tablespoons
　mayonnaise (see page 19)
salt and pepper
1 tablespoon lemon juice
　(strained)
½ level teaspoon ground
　cumin
pinch curry powder
few drops Tabasco sauce

MIX THE CREAM and mayonnaise (bought mayonnaise is ideal for this dip). Stir in salt, pepper, lemon juice, cumin, curry powder and a few drops of Tabasco sauce to taste. Serve with raw vegetables.
Serves 8

Sweet and Sour Chops

6 spare rib pork chops
salt and pepper

Sweet and Sour Sauce:
8 tablespoons clear honey
6 tablespoons soy sauce
6 tablespoons tomato ketchup
½ level teaspoon mustard
  powder
½ level teaspoon paprika
few drops Tabasco sauce
1 garlic clove (crushed)
½ level teaspoon salt
¼ pint white wine vinegar
¼ pint fresh orange juice
  (strained)

WIPE THE CHOPS and season with salt and pepper. Grill under a hot grill until nicely browned on both sides. Combine all the sauce ingredients and whisk well. Transfer the chops to a roasting tin, cover with the sauce and cook for about 1 hour 15 minutes or until tender at Gas 4/350°F.
Serves 6

Guacamole

2 large avocados (peeled)
2 tablespoons lemon juice
  (strained)
1 level teaspoon onion (finely
  grated)
3 level tablespoons soured
  cream
salt and pepper

REMOVE THE AVOCADO stones and mash the flesh with the lemon juice, onion, soured cream and salt and pepper to taste. Serve with crisps.
Serves 8

Spice Cake

6 ounces plain flour
1 level teaspoon baking
  powder
½ level teaspoon ground
  nutmeg
½ level teaspoon ground
  ginger
½ level teaspoon ground
  cinnamon
½ level teaspoon ground
  allspice
3 ounces margarine
4 level tablespoons golden
  syrup
1 large egg (beaten)

SIFT THE FLOUR with the baking powder and spices. Cream the margarine until soft and fluffy, then add the syrup and beat well. Beat in the egg thoroughly. Fold in the flour mixture, sultanas, lemon rind and juice and milk to give a fairly stiff dropping consistency.

Turn the mixture into a greased and paper-lined 6-inch cake tin, preferably with a loose bottom. Bake for about 1½ hours at Gas 3/325°F. Allow to cool for 30 minutes in the tin, then turn the cake out on to a wire rack to finish cooling.

10 ounces sultanas
rind of 1 lemon (grated)
juice of ½ lemon (strained)
2 tablespoons milk

Yoghurt Dressing

½ garlic clove (crushed)
2 level teaspoons made
  mustard
1 tablespoon lemon juice
  (strained)
salt and pepper
2 5-ounce cartons natural yoghurt
4 level tablespoons parsley (chopped)

Combine all ingredients, chill and serve with green or
mixed salads.
Serves 8

Tomato Soup

2 pounds very ripe tomatoes
  (quartered)
salt and pepper
1 pint chicken stock
1 level teaspoon caster sugar
2 ounces Cheddar cheese
  (grated)

PUT THE TOMATOES and seasoning in a large saucepan.
Cover with a tightly-fitting lid and cook over a very
low heat for about 20 minutes until really soft. Push the
tomatoes through a sieve and return the purée to the
rinsed pan. Add the chicken stock and sugar to taste.
Bring to the boil, taste for seasoning, then serve garnished
with the grated cheese.
Serves 6

Spiced Nuts

2 ounces whole hazelnuts
2 ounces flaked almonds
2 ounces whole peanuts
3 ounces walnuts (chopped)
1 garlic clove (crushed)
2 ounces butter
3 ounces sultanas
2 ounces currants
1 level teaspoon ground
  cinnamon
½ level teaspoon ground
  cumin
1 level tablespoon parsley
  (chopped)

PUT THE NUTS, garlic and butter in a frying-pan and
fry the nuts, stirring all the time, for about 5 minutes.
Stir in the sultanas, currants, cinnamon, cumin and
parsley. Allow to cool and serve as an appetiser.
Serves 8

Baked Potatoes with Cream and Chives

8 large potatoes
salt and pepper
5-ounce carton soured cream
1 tablespoon chives (snipped)

WASH AND SCRUB the potatoes and wrap each one in
foil. Push into the ashes of your fire or put on top of the
grid of the barbecue. Leave for at least 1 hour or until
soft when squeezed. Open the foil, slit the tops of the
potatoes and sprinkle with salt and pepper. Stir the
cream and chives together and spoon some into each
potato. Serve from the foil.
Serves 8

Hamburgers

1 large onion (chopped)
1 small egg (beaten)
¾ pound raw minced beef
salt and pepper
1 large onion (sliced)
4 ounces dripping or lard
4 soft rolls
tomato ketchup

MIX THE CHOPPED onion and egg into the minced beef with plenty of salt and pepper to season. Separate the onion slices into rings. Melt the dripping or lard in a large frying-pan. Fry the onion rings gently for about 5 minutes or until soft and golden brown. Meanwhile, form the meat into 4 flat cakes. Fry the hamburgers for about 10 minutes, turning once or twice. Cook for about 7 minutes if you like them rare and about 12 minutes if you prefer really well-done meat.

Split each roll and fill with a hamburger, some fried onion rings and tomato ketchup. Wrap in a paper napkin and serve or stack quickly in a basket to hand round.
Serves 8

Black Forest Sparkler

1 bottle cider
15-ounce can cherries
1 heaped tablespoon soft
  brown sugar
1 level dessertspoon ground
  cinnamon
¼ pint cherry brandy

POUR THE CIDER into a large pan with the cherries and their juice, the sugar and cinnamon. Bring very slowly almost to boiling point. Pour into a serving bowl or jug, stir in the cherry brandy and serve at once.
Serves 10

Golden Fizz

15-ounce can pineapple
  tidbits
2 ounces sultanas
½ pint sweet sherry
1 bottle dry cider
1 bottle soda water

EMPTY THE PINEAPPLE into a serving bowl and put in the fridge to chill. Soak the sultanas in the sherry and put with the bottles of cider and soda water to chill for at least 1 hour. Pour sherry, sultanas, soda and cider into the pineapple. Stir lightly and serve immediately.
Serves 10

Toddlers' Parties

I WISH TODDLERS' PARTIES were as easy to organise as they seem to be. I suppose it's the thought of not one fussy eater but five or six that puts the average mum into a tiz just thinking about the event. I don't think it matters if they don't eat—they're usually too excited to do more than pick anyway. As soon as a toddler has one thing on his plate, he sees something else and boredom sets in with what he's already got. A toddler's interest is easy to catch, hard to keep, so food can be perfectly ordinary but dressed up to be more eye-catching than usual and appear quite different. A cake must be the centrepiece because blowing out the right number of candles will be an indispensable ritual. The shape of the cake isn't important though most toddlers will be more excited by a novelty cake rather than just a plain square or round one. If you haven't got the right kind of fingers to cope with making a miniature zoo, dolls' tea party or whatever is the favourite idea of the moment, look out for party-cake kits in the shops. In a box you get everything to turn your cake into a football pitch, teddy bears' picnic and so on, saving you the trouble of thinking it out yourself.

Savouries should be tiny, scaled down to the toddlers' size. Miniature sandwiches, cut into animal shapes, should be filled with vegetable extract, sandwich spread, fish pastes, cheese or chocolate spreads, peanut butter or mashed banana or anything else which isn't going to ooze or fall out or otherwise make a mess. Children love personal things so they'll be delighted if you label a cake each for them using paper drinking straws, perhaps the ones that look like barbers' poles, with a sticky-label flag attached and pushed into the sponge. Or you could pipe the names directly on to the cakes if you've got a steady hand.

Drinks should be simple—squashes in beakers or non-breakable glasses with straws. Provide lots of alternatives and toddlers become confused. You'll find dozens of just-sipped drinks all over the place.

It's essential to cover your table, particularly if it's a good one, with a large sheet of polythene and then with a paper tablecloth. There are some marvellous designs about. I've seen them with delightful ragamuffins, Disney characters and with Santa Claus for Christmas. Also on sale are Mickey Mouse and ragamuffin table decorations. Provide paper cups to match if you like, although for toddlers I find their lack of sturdiness is a problem.

Although it's pleasing to set everything out on the table as you would for an adult party, it's bad for the children. They'll eat the biscuits and sweets, leave the sandwiches and end up feeling ill. Put on the savouries, then bring on the sweet items after a certain amount of eating has already taken place. Finally, carry in the cake and light the candles ready for the birthday child to blow them out and make a special wish.

Games are very important to toddlers, though they can make or break a party. I like to get some rowdy games over at first to let off high spirits, then go on to some thinking games just before tea. Rowdy games include blind man's buff, musical chairs, pass the parcel and hunt the gifts (hidden round the room). Thinking games include I-spy, putting on the donkey's tail and guessing games—though even these can be extremely noisy. After tea I usually plan on the quiet games and I read a story, or better still tell a story and act out the parts. Dressing up and acting out a fairy tale comes into this category.

Two hours seems ample time for a toddlers' party, though as the children get older (nearer the age of five), three hours would be fine. How long the party lasts seems to be a cross between what you can stand in the way of noise and the other extreme of sending over-excited and hysterical children back to their parents; though when they're tiny, you often have the moral support of the parents to help you through the party.

Keep masses of tissues handy. A bowl of damp facecloths is marvellous too for keeping fingers sticky with chocolate and jam off the furniture and carpets.

Give each child a small gift to take home. You can buy those old-fashioned sweetie bags—the kind with the drawstrings—at most stationers and these can be filled with different sweets and tiny toys like squeakers, puzzles, whistles, plastic snakes and other things to delight the children and irritate their parents.

While tiny children can't be expected to help much with the clearing up, I think there are all kinds of little things they can do to help arrange the party. Little ones can colour plain paper doilies or make their own. Show them how first of all by folding a piece of paper in half, then quarters, then eighths and cutting off the corners to make a rough circle. Small holes, diamonds, squares and circles can be cut and when opened out a rough but home-made doily results. Children can cut the sandwiches into animal shapes. Make them the day before to allow for the delays while the little ones cut and cover the sandwiches with a damp cloth over-night to keep them moist. You could also ask them to cut out pretty pictures to be used as placemarkers. Give tiny children a tray of little sponge buns and a plate full of silver balls, hundreds and thousands, sugar flowers and tiny sweets and let them decorate the buns themselves.

Snowballs

2 large egg whites
5 ounces caster sugar
5 ounces desiccated coconut
6 tablespoons apricot jam
4 ounces long thread coconut

WHISK THE EGG whites stiffly, then fold in the sugar and desiccated coconut using a tablespoon. Press the mixture into lightly greased shallow egg cups and turn out on to greased baking sheets covered with rice paper. Bake for about 45 minutes or until just coloured at Gas ½/250°F. Cool. Sandwich 2 halves together with jam, then spread jam lightly round the outsides and roll in the long thread coconut to coat completely. Put in paper cases and decorate if liked with pieces of glacé cherry and angelica.
Makes 10

Banana Rolls

6 large bananas (firm)
juice of 1 lemon (strained)
Demerara sugar
1 large brown loaf
6 ounces butter (softened)

CUT EACH BANANA into 3 pieces, then cut each piece in half lengthways. Dip each piece in lemon juice to keep it white, then roll it in Demerara sugar to coat well. Cut the crusts off the loaf and cut into slices lengthways, making 12 long slices in all. Butter the bread. Cut each slice into three. Roll a piece of banana in each piece of bread and arrange with the cut ends underneath to secure. Cover with a damp cloth until ready to serve.
Makes 36

Birthday Express

8 chocolate mini rolls
liquorice allsorts
wooden cocktail sticks
liquorice bootlaces
1 ounce butter (creamed)
2 ounces icing sugar (sifted)
jelly babies
candles

UNWRAP THE CHOCOLATE mini rolls. Push the large round coconut liquorice allsorts sweets on to either end of wooden cocktail sticks to form the wheels of the carriages. Stand a mini roll on two sets of these wheels. Arrange the liquorice bootlaces as rails on a silver cake board, a wooden tray or a chopping board. Beat the butter and icing sugar together and use tiny dabs of this icing to stick the bootlaces on to the board. Use icing to stick one of the black liquorice allsorts sweets on to one mini roll as the engine funnel. Push short pieces of bootlace into each mini roll to join the carriages together. Arrange the carriages on the bootlace rails.

Stand jelly babies around the train, sticking them with dabs of icing. Cut some liquorice allsorts into small pieces for the luggage. Spread a thin layer of icing over the top of the 7 carriages and stick the luggage in place. Push the required number of candles (8 in this case, or make more carriages to suit the number of guests in the party) into the carriages and engine.
Serves 8

Rose Cream Fizz

4 tablespoons rose hip syrup
4 tablespoons strawberry
  ice cream
1 small bottle soda water

PUT THE ROSE hip syrup and ice cream into 4 tall glasses. Top up with the soda water, stir to mix and serve with straws and long spoons.
Serves 4

Funny-Face Cup Cakes

2 ounces margarine
2 ounces caster sugar
1 standard egg (beaten)
2 ounces self-raising flour
1 level dessertspoon cocoa
milk to mix
chocolate glacé icing (see page 45)
coloured sugar-coated chocolate sweets
glacé cherries
chocolate buttons

CREAM THE MARGARINE and caster sugar until light and fluffy. Beat in the egg thoroughly, then fold in the flour sifted with the cocoa. Mix to a soft dropping consistency with the milk. Divide the mixture between 12 paper cases arranged in tartlet tins. Bake for about 10 minutes at Gas 5/375°F. Cool on a wire rack.

Pour glacé icing over each bun to give a good thick covering. Sort the sweets into different faces, using the coloured sweets for eyes and mouth, glacé cherries for mouth, chocolate buttons, cut in halves or quarters across, for eyebrows and any chocolate bits for the hair or use a crumbled flake bar for the hair. Arrange on the cup cakes and leave to set.
Makes 12

Chocolate Trifles

1 chocolate Swiss roll
15-ounce can strawberries
15-ounce can peach slices
1 ounce cornflour
1 level tablespoon caster sugar
1 pint milk
2 level tablespoons drinking chocolate
¼ pint double cream
chocolate buttons

CUT THE SWISS roll into 8 slices and put a slice in each of 8 individual dishes or arrange in a large bowl. Strain the fruit and pour the strawberry syrup over the Swiss roll to moisten. You may have to use some of the peach syrup as well. Cover with the mixed fruit. Blend the cornflour and caster sugar with a little of the milk. Put the remainder on to heat. When almost boiling, whisk in the drinking chocolate and pour it on to the cornflour mixture. Stir well and return to the heat, and simmer gently for 3 minutes. Stir in 1 tablespoon cream and cool slightly, stirring often to prevent a skin forming. Pour over the trifle and allow to set. Whip the remaining cream and put it into a piping bag fitted with a large star nozzle. Pipe stars around the large trifle (one for each child) or pipe a large rosette in the centre of each individual trifle. Decorate with chocolate buttons.
Serves 8

Catherine Wheels

1 large brown loaf
6 ounces butter (softened)
6 ounces cream cheese

CUT THE CRUSTS off the loaf and cut into slices lengthways. Butter each slice generously, then spread with the cream cheese. Roll each slice from one short end and stand rolls on their cut ends or secure with cocktail sticks or wrap in greaseproof paper, twisting the ends like sweet papers. Chill in the fridge for 1 hour. Remove and cut into thin slices.
Makes 48

Frankfurter Rolls

8 frankfurter sausages
8 slices thin brown bread
2 ounces butter (softened)

HEAT THE SAUSAGES according to the directions on the tin. Cut the crusts off the bread and butter slices generously. When sausages are cool roll each one tightly in a buttered slice and arrange with ends underneath to secure. Or secure with cocktail sticks until the party.
Serves 8

Sandwich Zoo

butter (softened)
1 large white loaf (thinly sliced)
1 large brown loaf (thinly sliced)
peanut butter
sandwich spread
vegetable extract
cheese spread
chocolate spread
2 large bananas (mashed)
2 level teaspoons Demerara sugar

SPREAD BUTTER ON an equal number of white and brown slices of bread. Spread with peanut butter, sandwich spread, vegetable extract, cheese or chocolate spread. Mix the bananas and sugar and use for more slices of bread. Cut each sandwich into 2 animal shapes using animal cutters. It's easier if you leave the crusts on the bread and cut out the centres. Label each lot of sandwiches clearly, using paper drinking straws cut to the length required with sticky-label flags attached, bearing the name of the flavour.
Makes 40

Spider's Webs

9 ounces butter
6 ounces caster sugar
3 large eggs (beaten)
6 ounces self-raising flour
6 ounces icing sugar (sifted)

CREAM 6 OUNCES butter with the caster sugar until light and fluffy. Gradually beat in the eggs, then fold in the flour. Turn the mixture into 2 8-inch round sandwich tins and bake for about 25 minutes at Gas 5/375°F. Cool on wire racks.

2 ounces walnuts (chopped)
glacé icing (see page 46)
cocoa

Cream the remaining butter and icing sugar together. Cut the cooled cakes into 2-inch rounds using a plain cutter. Spread ⅔ of the butter cream round the sides of each cake and roll in the chopped nuts. Run glacé icing on top of each cake and allow to set. Beat cocoa powder into the reserved butter cream to give a good brown colour. Put into a paper piping bag. Pipe a spider's web on top of each cake.
Makes 20

Jam Cushions

4 ounces butter
4 ounces caster sugar
1 large egg (beaten)
8 ounces plain flour
pinch salt
raspberry jam
lemon curd
icing sugar

CREAM THE BUTTER and caster sugar until light and fluffy. Beat in the egg, then mix in the flour to make a smooth firm dough. If the dough seems a little too soft to roll, wrap it in greaseproof paper and leave it in the fridge for 30 minutes. Roll the dough on a lightly floured surface to ⅛-inch thickness. Cut out rounds using a 2½-inch fluted cutter. Cut out the centres of half the biscuits using a 1-inch fluted cutter. Arrange the biscuits on greased baking sheets and bake for about 15 minutes at Gas 4/350°F. Cool on wire racks. When cool, spread the complete biscuits with jam or lemon curd. Sift icing sugar over the ring biscuits and carefully sandwich with the jam-covered biscuits. Fill the centres with a little more jam if necessary to make a nice cushion.
Makes 10

Little Candle Cakes

1 bought plain Swiss roll
4 tablespoons strawberry
    jam
glacé icing (see page 46)
cochineal
liquorice bootlaces
8 candles

CUT THE SWISS roll into 16 thin slices and sandwich them in pairs with the strawberry jam. Make the glacé icing into a flowing consistency and add a few drops of cochineal to turn it into a pale pink. Stand the cakes on a wire rack over a Swiss roll tin. Pour the icing over the cakes to coat them completely. Leave to set. Gather up the icing from the Swiss roll tin and if necessary make the icing into a flowing consistency again. Add another coat to the cakes. Cut the liquorice bootlaces into lengths and push them into the icing to form the handles of the candle-holders. Push a candle into the centre of each cake and light all before bringing them to the table.
Makes 8

Log Cabin

8 ounces margarine
8 ounces caster sugar
4 large eggs (beaten)
8 ounces self-raising flour
4 ounces butter
1 pound icing sugar (sifted)
2–3 tablespoons strawberry
   milk shake syrup
chocolate finger biscuits
liquorice allsorts
1 large egg white
few drops glycerine
granulated sugar
rosemary sprigs
small figures and animals

CREAM THE MARGARINE and caster sugar until light and fluffy. Beat in the eggs, beating well after each addition, then fold in the flour. Turn the mixture into a greased 8-inch square cake tin which should be lined on the base with greaseproof paper. Bake the cake for about 45 minutes at Gas 5/375°F. Allow to cool on a wire rack.

Cream the butter until very pale. Gradually beat in 8 ounces icing sugar and the strawberry milk shake syrup. Cut a piece off the cake measuring 3 inches wide by 8 inches. Cut this oblong into 2 wedges, cutting from 1 long edge, diagonally through the cake to the opposite long edge. Turn one wedge upside down so the short sides of the wedges are together. Spread butter icing along one side of one wedge and stick the other to it. This will give you the roof for assembly and decoration. Spread icing on the big piece and put the roof in place. It should have a slight overhang.

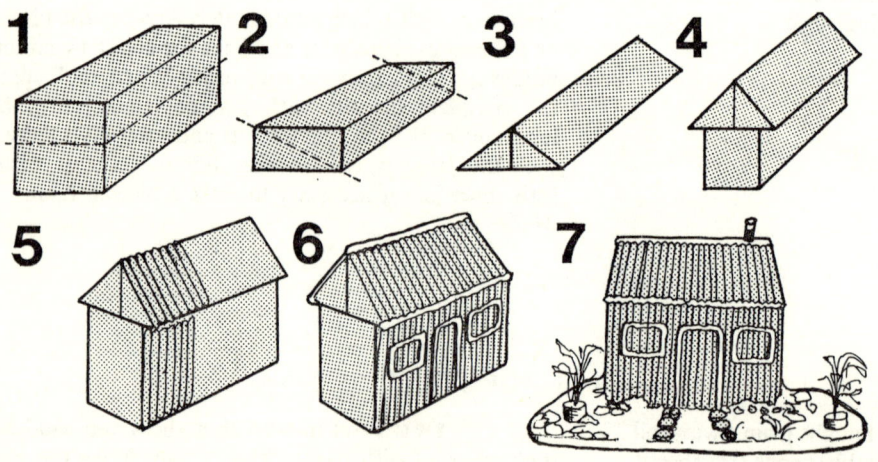

Spread icing along the sides of the cabin and stick the finger biscuits in place. Spread icing along the roof and cover with finger biscuits, letting them come right to the edge of the roof. If they don't quite meet at the top of the roof, this join can be filled in later with icing. Cut a V-shape from 1 thick liquorice allsorts sandwich to fit the roof and form the chimney. Stick another 1 or 2 allsorts on top to make a tall chimney. Stick the chimney in place.

Whisk the egg white then gradually beat in the remaining icing sugar and glycerine, beating until the icing is thick and white and glossy. Put a third in a piping bag and pipe along the roof join to look like snow, piping a little icing into the crevices between the biscuits to make it look realistic. Pipe along the eaves of the roof, again letting the piping drip a little like icicles. Pipe windows and doors and pipe windowsills with piles of snow on them. Spread the remaining icing over a square cake board. Put the log cabin in the centre and smooth a path to the door, piling the icing on either side of the path with the piping bag. Add some snow to the chimney. Push candles into the snow round the log cabin. When the icing has dried on the board, sprinkle with the granulated sugar, which will sparkle if you turn down the lights. Push rosemary sprigs into large coconut allsorts to look like trees and arrange around the house. Complete with small figures and animals.

Little Jellies

1 packet strawberry jelly
1 packet lime jelly
1 packet lemon jelly
5-ounce carton double cream
miniature jelly sweets

MAKE UP EACH jelly according to the directions on the packet and pour into the cartons left from bought mousses (those with a pretty shape to them). Allow to set. Turn out the jellies on to saucers. Whisk the cream with 1 tablespoon cold water until stiff. Put into a piping bag and pipe stars on top of each jelly and around the sides. Decorate each cream star with a tiny jelly sweet. *Serves 12*

Animal Roundabout

8-inch round sponge cake
  (see page 76)
8 ounces butter
1 pound icing sugar (sifted)
chocolate vermicelli
2 paper drinking straws
narrow red ribbon
cochineal
red sugar-coated chocolate
  sweets
chocolate animals

MAKE AND BAKE the sponge and allow to cool completely on a wire rack. Cream the butter until light and fluff, then beat in the icing sugar. Use a little to sandwich the two cakes together. Spread one third around the sides of the cake and smooth using a palette knife. Holding the top and bottom of the cake, roll the sides in the chocolate vermicelli to coat.

Using the 2 straws together, wrap the ribbon round to cover and glue at the top. Make 6 or 8 ribbon streamers and glue to the top of the pole. Cover the top of the cake with one third of the icing and smooth with the palette knife. Push the straws into the centre of the cake. Colour the remaining icing pale pink using cochineal and spoon it into a piping bag fitted with a small star nozzle. Pipe stars around the top edge of the cake and decorate each star with a red sweet. Arrange the ribbons out to the sides and stand a chocolate animal on each one securing it upright with stars of icing. Pipe stars around the base of the cake and decorate with red sweets.

Children's Parties

ONCE CHILDREN ARE over the toddler stage their parties become much easier because they have developed strong ideas about what they like and dislike and about what kinds of food fall into the category of treats to be provided for a party. The answers can be quite surprising when you ask them what they want—sausages on sticks seeming to be the height of special-occasion foods, closely followed by crisps and things like toffee apples, cheese straws, bought mousses—in fact anything bought nowadays seems to rate higher than the home-made variety; such is the power of television commercials.

However, it seems best to ignore most of what the children say and provide for them the usual well-balanced tea, some savouries and some sweets, though not as many sweets as they'd like. But as with toddlers, dress everything up to look exciting and very special. The party rules for toddlers apply to parties for older children. It's essential to cover the table with a large piece of plastic and it saves time and temper if you use a paper tablecloth. Paper cups are fine for this age group, but of course, they're less likely to drop things anyway, so sturdy kitchen tumblers won't come to harm—as long as you don't mind washing them up afterwards.

Of course, they'll get excited and being larger can rampage all the more noisily and effectively than toddlers. It isn't easy to wear this age group out by letting them loose in the garden with a water pistol each, and they'll think you're soft if you suggest a quiet game before tea. Boys should be smartly organised into two teams as soon as they arrive with team leaders, one of whom should be the birthday boy. You can set up a little rivalry between the teams if table manners are forgotten or if there is too much rowdiness. You can organise games like football and cricket or whatever is the passion of the moment. Bursting balloons has never failed me. I fling dozens from an upstairs window, telling the children they must try and keep one for themselves intact while bursting as many of the others as possible. Proof of burst balloons must be the small piece of string and the neck of the balloon. There should be a prize for the person who's managed to keep a balloon intact to the last moment and one for the person who's managed to burst the most balloons. It's worth remembering that children of this age don't go in for what's fair or realise that people who get prizes have worked for them. Either provide on any kind of excuse a small prize for everyone or be prepared to put up with a few tears from someone who doesn't think it fair that he hasn't got a pencil or whistle or whatever. I'm inclined to let the parents take care of their child's attitude to life and provide a prize for everyone for the sake of the peace and quiet.

It's perfectly possible to split the tea for boys who can go on eating indefinitely. I put on the savouries first and when these seem to be finished, get the children into the garden or another room while I clear and bring on the sweets and cake.

Girls can be much easier because they're usually quieter and not so difficult to control. But split the tea again; I reckon it makes life easier for the mum organising the party. Girls and boys of this age can actually help get the food ready. They should be able to make small buns themselves and biscuits, but even if you haven't trusted them with this kind of job, they can ice and decorate very well. Get them doing this the day before the party because they'll be very slow, liking to take a long time over it. Sandwiches are best filled with spreads and pastes as for the toddlers—fillings such as peanut butter, mashed bananas or chocolate spread don't fall out and have the added advantage of holding the bread together so there won't be so many crumbs to sweep up afterwards.

Three hours is long enough for a party, particularly as children rate the success of a party not by the length of time it has lasted but by the amount of loot they've managed to collect. You could name a place for each child by putting a small parcel on the plate with a tiny gift inside, to be opened after the sandwiches have been eaten. You could make a cake like a large toy basket, covering the top with a piece of cardboard cut to size and piling tiny toys on it—squeakers, notebooks, pencils, puzzles, small books, games, ping pong balls and so on. But put a name on each one to prevent fights breaking out as they snatch them from the top of the cake.

Set a definite time for the party to end, otherwise, like bedtime, it tends to get later and later. It's always helpful if one parent says he'll collect his offspring because this can be the start of getting the rest of them together with their coats, loot, pieces of cake to take home and other prizes and presents they've won, scrounged or swopped.

Of course you can avoid all this by taking the children to see the latest Disney adventure at the cinema or on some other treat, just bringing them back to the house for the tea. This is costly, though. Cheaper entertainments for boys include football matches, and fun fairs always appeal if there's one about at the time.

Lemonade

4 large lemons
6 ounces caster sugar
1 pint boiling water

THINLY PEEL THE rind from 3 lemons, discarding any bitter white pith. Put into a large jug with the sugar and pour on the boiling water. Squeeze and strain juice from peeled lemons and stir into lemonade. Chill. Thinly slice remaining lemon and float slices on top.
Serves 6

Milk Shakes

8 tablespoons vanilla ice
    cream
raspberry milk shake syrup
2 pints milk (chilled)

PUT THE ICE cream and about 6 or 8 tablespoons milk shake syrup into a blender. Top up with the milk and blend until the mixture is frothy. Pour into tall glasses and serve at once.
Serves 8

Coca-Cola Float

4 individual bricks vanilla
    ice cream
2 bottles Coca-Cola

CUT THE ICE cream into 8 portions and put one in each of 8 tall glasses. Pour on Coca-Cola slowly and serve at once with straws and long spoons.
Serves 8

Sausage Rolls

8-ounce packet frozen
    shortcrust pastry
8 ounces beef sausagemeat
plain flour
1 large egg (beaten)

ALLOW THE PASTRY to thaw at room temperature for at least 1 hour. Roll out to a large oblong about 6 inches by 12 inches on a lightly floured board. Cut the oblong in half lengthways. Form the sausagemeat into two rolls, each 12 inches long, flouring your hands when they become sticky. Put one sausagemeat roll down the length of each pastry strip. Moisten one edge of each with water and fold over. Press edges well to seal and decorate with the prongs of a fork. Using a sharp knife, cut the rolls into 1-inch lengths. Brush with egg and bake for about 25 minutes at Gas 6/400°F.
Makes 20–24

Fish Finger Hot Dogs

8 fish fingers
8 soft long rolls
4 level tablespoons sandwich
    spread
2 tomatoes (sliced)
salt and pepper

GRILL THE FISH fingers for about 10 minutes turning them once. Spread the cut rolls with the sandwich spread and fill each roll with 1 fish finger and some tomato slices. Season with salt and pepper and serve at once.
Serves 8

Cheese and Pineapple Tarts

8 ounces plain flour
pinch salt
4 ounces margarine
4 ounces Cheddar cheese
   (grated)
8-ounce can pineapple pieces
1 level teaspoon arrowroot
5-ounce carton cream cheese
cayenne pepper
milk

SIFT THE FLOUR and salt into a bowl. Rub in the margarine. Stir in the cheese and mix to a stiff dough with cold water. Roll out on a lightly floured board and use to line 24 tartlet tins, using a 2½-inch fluted cutter. Prick the base of each tartlet and fill with baking beans. Bake for 10 minutes at Gas 6/400°F. then remove the beans and bake for 5 minutes more if necessary to crisp and brown the pastry. Cool on wire racks.

Strain the pineapple and blend the arrowroot with a little of the juice. Bring the remainder to the boil. Pour a little on to the blended arrowroot, stir well. Return to the pan, bring to the boil, stirring all the time, and cook for 2 minutes while the sauce thickens and clears. Allow to cool, stirring occasionally. Arrange pineapple pieces in each of the tartlet cases. Mash the cream cheese to a piping consistency, adding the cayenne pepper and a little milk if necessary. Put into a piping bag fitted with a small star nozzle. Spoon a little pineapple glaze over each tartlet case and pipe cream cheese round the edge for decoration.
Makes 24

Egg Boats

8-ounce packet frozen
   shortcrust pastry
4 hard-boiled eggs
salt and pepper
4 level tablespoons sandwich
   spread
2 tomatoes

ALLOW THE PASTRY to thaw at room temperature for at least 1 hour. Roll out on a lightly floured board and use to line 15 boat tins. Fill with baking beans and bake for about 10 minutes at Gas 6/400°F., then remove the beans and bake for another 5 minutes if necessary to crisp and brown the pastry. Allow to cool on wire racks.

Mash the eggs with salt and pepper and the sandwich spread. Use to fill the boats. Cut the tomatoes into thin wedges and put a wedge on each boat. Cut sails from foil if liked and thread a wooden cocktail stick through each one to hold. Push the stick into the pastry. Set sail on lettuce leaves.
Makes 15

Fish Finger Bites

10 fish fingers
15 small pickled onions
5 ounces Cheddar cheese
1 red eating apple

GRILL THE FISH fingers under a medium grill until golden brown on both sides. Allow to cool completely, then cut each one into 3 pieces. Stick a piece on to 15 cocktail sticks and add an onion to each one. Cut the cheese into 15 pieces the same size as the fish fingers.

Put a piece of fish and a piece of cheese on another 15 cocktail sticks. Push the sticks into the eating apple. You may have to cut a piece off the base of the apple to make it stand flat.
Makes 30

Ice Cream with Butterscotch Sauce

1 family-size block vanilla ice cream
2 ounces butter
2 ounces Demerara sugar
1 heaped tablespoon golden syrup
2 ounces almond nibs (toasted)
2 teaspoons lemon juice (strained)

SCOOP THE ICE cream into 8 glasses but leave them in the ice-making compartment of the fridge until you're ready to serve.

Heat the butter, sugar and syrup until they're well blended. Bring to the boil and boil for 1 minute. Stir in the nuts and lemon juice. Pour over the ice cream and serve at once.

Or serve with hot chocolate sauce (see page 34).
Serves 8

Cheese Straws

8 ounces plain flour
pinch salt
4 ounces margarine
4 ounces Cheddar cheese (grated)
cayenne pepper

SIFT THE FLOUR and salt into a bowl. Rub in the margarine, then stir in the cheese and mix to a stiff dough with cold water. Roll out on a lightly floured board. Cut into strips about ¼ inch wide, then cut strips into 3-inch lengths. Arrange on lightly greased baking sheets and bake for about 10 minutes or until crisp at Gas 7/425°F. Sprinkle with cayenne pepper while still warm. Cool on wire racks. Arrange in bundles, tied with paper drinking straws.

Ring Doughnuts

1 pound self-raising flour
pinch salt
8 ounces caster sugar
6 ounces soft margarine
2 large eggs (beaten)
milk to mix
oil or fat for deep frying
ground nutmeg

SIFT THE FLOUR and salt into a bowl. Stir in 2 ounces sugar. Rub in the margarine and mix to a stiff dough with the eggs and milk. Roll out on a lightly floured board to a ¼-inch thickness and cut into rounds using a 3-inch plain cutter. Cut out the centres of each doughnut using a 1-inch plain cutter. Deep fry for about 5 minutes until golden brown and well risen. Drain on kitchen paper. Mix the remaining sugar with 1 heaped teaspoon ground nutmeg and toss the doughnuts in this mixture to coat well.
Makes 20

Hansel and Gretel Cottage

8-inch square sponge cake
(see page 78)
butter icing (see page 79)
barley sugar sticks
peppermint creams
coloured sugar-coated
chocolate sweets
white chocolate bars
hundreds and thousands
royal icing (see page 78)
sugar flowers
silver balls
granulated sugar

MAKE AND BAKE the sponge cake and cut and shape into a house using some of the butter icing (see page 78). Use some of the icing to stick the cake to a 9-inch silver cake board. Using the remaining butter icing, cover the house with sweets like the Witch's house in Hansel and Gretel using barley sugar sticks for the corners of the house, halves of peppermint creams for the eaves of the roof, sugar-coated chocolate sweets for the roof and white chocolate bars cut into shape for the windows and doors. Hundreds and thousands can be used for the walls of the house.

Using the royal icing, stick sugar flowers around the doors and windows of the house and silver balls between the sugar-coated sweets on the roof. Coat the board with the rest of the icing. Sprinkle with granulated sugar and allow to dry. Finish with the figures of a small boy and girl if liked and pile sweets around the house.

Jelly Slices

4 large oranges
1 packet orange jelly
1 packet lime jelly

CUT EACH ORANGE in half and squeeze out and strain the juice. Using a teaspoon, scoop out all the flesh and discard. Make up the jellies according to the packet directions but use the orange juice in place of some of the water to make the orange jelly. Pour jelly into the orange halves and leave to set. When completely set, cut into quarters using a sharp knife and arrange the jelly quarters on a plate, alternating the colours. Decorate with cocktail stick masts and foil sails.
Makes 16

Toffee Apples

8 large apples
8 wooden sticks
1 pound Demerara sugar
2 ounces butter
2 teaspoons vinegar
2 level tablespoons golden
syrup
¼ pint cold water

WIPE THE APPLES and push the sticks into the cores securely. Wooden skewers from the butcher are good but old lolly sticks will do. Put the sugar, butter, vinegar, syrup and water in a pan with a heavy base. Heat gently until the sugar has dissolved. Do not stir. Boil rapidly for about 5 minutes or until the temperature has reached 290°F. Dip the apples in the toffee, twirl around as you lift each one out; plunge it into iced water and leave to harden on a lightly greased baking sheet.
Makes 8

Hot Sausages with Ketchup

1 pound chipolata sausages
1 green apple
ketchup

TWIST EACH SAUSAGE in half to make two small sausages. Arrange them in a roasting tin and cook for about 30 minutes at Gas 6/400°F. Drain well and stick a wooden cocktail stick into each one. Push each cocktail stick into the apple. It may be necessary to cut a slice off the base of the apple to make it stand. Put on a saucer. Put a small bowl of ketchup nearby.

Makes 20

Daleks

4 ounces soft margarine
4 ounces caster sugar
2 large eggs (beaten)
4 ounces self-raising flour
chocolate fingers
4 ounces butter
8 ounces icing sugar (sifted)
green colouring
miniature jelly sweets

CREAM THE MARGARINE and caster sugar until light and fluffy. Beat in the eggs thoroughly, then fold in the sifted flour. Turn the mixture into 15 dariole moulds. Bake for about 10 minutes at Gas 5/375°F. Allow to cool a little then turn out of the moulds and finish cooling on a wire rack. Cut several chocolate fingers in half. Cream the butter until soft and light in colour, then beat in the icing sugar. Colour the icing pale green. Pile a little on top of each cake to round the top. Push halves of chocolate biscuit through this cream and into the sponge. Push 2 more halves in the front of the cakes to make the 'feelers.' Spread icing over the rest of the madeleines. Put the remainder into a piping bag and pipe 7 lines down each dalek to make it 8-sided. Push coloured jelly sweets into the icing in rows between these lines. Arrange on a board and pipe round the chocolate fingers if there is any icing left. This will secure them.

Makes 15

Gingerbread Men

2½ ounces golden syrup
2 ounces caster sugar
1 level teaspoon ground
  ginger
pinch nutmeg
2 ounces butter
2 level teaspoons bicarbonate
  of soda
8 ounces plain flour
pinch salt
1 large egg yolk

PUT THE SYRUP, sugar, ginger and nutmeg in a saucepan. Heat until the syrup is runny. Continue to heat, adding the butter cut into very small pieces and stirring all the time. Remove from the heat and stir in the bicarbonate of soda. Allow to cool a little. Sift the flour and salt and stir into the mixture with the egg yolk to make a stiff dough. Knead well. Turn on to a floured board and roll out to ¼-inch thickness. Cut into 8 or 9 shapes using a gingerbread man cutter. Arrange on greased baking sheets and bake for about 20 minutes at Gas 4/350°F. Cool on wire racks. Decorate if liked when cold with glacé icing and silver balls.

Makes 8 or 9

Teddy Bears' Picnic

8-inch sponge cake (see
  page 76)
  or 8-inch bought sponge
8 ounces apricot jam
butter icing (see page 79)
  page 79)
3 ounces chocolate, melted
1 pound bought marzipan
silver balls
chocolate buttons

MAKE AND BAKE the cake, or use a bought sponge. If home-made, cut the cake in half and fill with apricot jam. If bought, sandwich if necessary. Beat icing and chocolate together and spread all over the cake. Using a fork, peak the icing round the sides and smooth the top using a palette knife. On a board sprinkled with icing sugar, roll the marzipan to $\frac{1}{4}$-inch thickness. Cut out lots of teddy bears, no bigger than the sides of the cake. Push silver balls into the teddy bears to form their eyes, nose and buttons on their bodies. Push the teddy bears into the icing round the cake so that their fingers just touch and form a circle. Push chocolate buttons into the spaces in between. Arrange teddy bears in the same way on the top of the cake. Pipe any remaining icing around the top edge of the cake and decorate with chocolate buttons.

Little Lace Cakes

4 ounces soft margarine
4 ounces caster sugar
2 large eggs (beaten)
4 ounces self-raising flour
8 ounces apricot conserve
glacé icing (see page 46)
green colouring
icing sugar
angelica leaves
glacé cherries

PUT THE MARGARINE, sugar, eggs and flour in a large bowl. Using a wooden spoon beat well for 3 minutes. Turn the mixture into 2 greased and floured 8-inch sandwich tins and bake for about 25 minutes at Gas 5/375°F. Cool a little in the tins, then turn on to a wire rack to cool completely. Cut each cooled cake into 2 layers and sandwich together again with the apricot conserve. Cut each cake into rounds using a 2-inch plain cutter. Use the remaining bits for a trifle or truffle cakes.

Colour the glacé icing pale green. Stand the cakes on a wire rack over a Swiss roll tin. Cover each cake with icing, then gather the drips from the tin and cover each cake with another coat of green icing. Allow to set. Cover each cake with a paper doily and dust with icing sugar. Lift off the doilies carefully to leave the lace patterns. Cut off the borders from some doilies and use to decorate the bottom edge of each cake, sticking the cut ends to the cake with a spot of glacé icing. Push angelica leaves into each cake and finish with a small piece of glacé cherry to look like a flower.
Makes 20

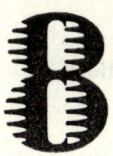

Teenagers' Parties

TEENAGERS PREFER A buffet to a meal for which they all sit down, which seems childish to them. Everything has to be as grown-up as possible, for this is the age where both boys and girls are trying desperately to be several years older all the time. If you feel you can trust your child or children, then it's a good idea to be out of the house for some part of the evening, coming back at 9 o'clock or even later. If you have to be around, let them have a room for the party so that it seems as if there's very little parental supervision. Certainly let them be on their own to eat.

Food for teenagers can be more substantial than the sort served at children's parties, with less emphasis on the sweet and sticky things so much loved by the little ones. It's still very important to make the party look interesting: party themes for this age-group are always successful. It's so easy to use a red check tablecloth and put on a cauldron of bangers and beans to give a Wild West theme, and plain sailing to keep the idea going with hamburgers and hot dogs, and drinks that look like moonshine but aren't.

The red check tablecloth can be used to give the party the setting of a little French bistro. You'll also need plenty of candles set in old wine bottles, preferably with plenty of candle grease dripped down the sides. This can be done easily if you burn a white household candle in each bottle the day before, then add a new candle for the party. Serve herb or garlic bread with baked potatoes, corn on the cob, baked chicken legs to be held in the fingers and dipped in various sauces. Cutlet frills should be used for the bone ends of the chicken.

Pizzas for an Italian party are easy to make, and easy to keep hot once cooked. Big bowls of spaghetti and tomato sauce make cheap party fare. Provide lots of grated cheese in another bowl to be sprinkled on by each guest. Old chianti bottles can hold the drink for the party, which could be a punch or plain cordial or just Coca-Cola or lemonade.

Setting up a hot-dog stall is another good idea for the teenage party. You need a heat tray at the back of the stall and large pans full of frankfurters, fried onions, hamburgers and so on. Provide another box of ready-cut rolls and guests can either help themselves or the party-giver can set up as proprietor. Don't forget to wrap the hot dogs in paper napkins—they're hot and greasy! Otherwise, remember that paper napkins, plates, cups, bowls and tablecloths are ideal for this age-group.

It really depends on what your own particular teenage offspring is like and what you know of their friends whether you treat them like children and put a large plastic covering over the table or assume they're adult enough to organise the whole buffet party for themselves. I don't see why they shouldn't do the greater part on their own. You can be near by to hand out advice and help.

If the weather's fine and your garden is large enough, give them a bonfire party. The time of the year doesn't really matter. Build a huge fire and let them take the food into the garden and sit round the fire to keep warm. They may like to cook several items in the ashes and there are numerous recipes and ideas in the barbecue section (Chapter 5) to satisfy this longing.

Set the time limit on the party fairly early—say, 10 o'clock—and insist that the clearing up be done by your children. And make sure that most of it is done on the night of the party, otherwise, unless you've used mostly paper tableware, you'll come down to breakfast and have to do a huge washing-up operation before you can make a cup of tea.

Pizza Napolitana

8 ounces plain flour
pinch salt
½ ounce fresh yeast or
¼ ounce dried yeast
¼ pint tepid water
8-ounce can tomatoes
good pinch dried basil
4 ounces mozzarella cheese
few anchovy fillets
few black olives

SIFT THE FLOUR and salt. If using fresh yeast, cream it with a little tepid water, then stir in the remainder. If using dried yeast, sprinkle it on the tepid water, leave for 15 minutes or until the liquid becomes frothy. Then use by making a well in the flour and pouring in either kind of yeast liquid. Mix to a dough then turn the dough on to a floured board and knead it well to distribute the yeast. Put the dough into a clean, lightly oiled bowl, cover with a damp cloth and leave in a warm place until doubled in size. When ready, the dough will be stringy when pulled from the sides of the bowl.

Turn the dough on to a floured board and knead well again for at least 5 minutes. Form the dough into a 10-inch round using your fingers and place on a lightly oiled baking sheet or 10-inch tin plate. Leave in a warm place to rise for about 20 minutes. Drain tomatoes and spread them over the dough, breaking them down if necessary with a fork. Sprinkle with basil. Slice the cheese and cover the tomatoes. Arrange the anchovies in a lattice pattern across the cheese and put an olive in

the centre of each square. Bake for 30 minutes at Gas
7/425°F. or until the edge is crisp and golden brown. Cut
in half to serve or make 2 small individual pizzas.
Serves 2

Cheese Extras

6 ounces plain flour
pinch salt
2 level teaspoons mustard
   powder
pinch paprika pepper
3 ounces butter
3 ounces Cheddar cheese
   (grated)
1 large egg yolk
beaten egg or milk to glaze

SIFT THE FLOUR with the salt, mustard and pepper.
Finely grate the butter into the bowl, straight from the
fridge. Stir in the cheese and mix to a firm dough with
the egg yolk mixed with a little cold water. Knead lightly
on a floured board and roll pastry to a square no more than
$\frac{3}{8}$ inch thick. Cut into $\frac{1}{2}$-inch wide strips. Arrange on
lightly greased baking sheets, twisting each strip as you
would for a lattice. Brush lightly with a little beaten egg
or milk and bake for about 10 minutes or until golden
brown and crisp at Gas 6/400°F. Allow to cool a little
on the baking sheets, then remove carefully on to wire
racks to cool completely.

Sweet and Sour Chicken

8 chicken drumsticks
2 tablespoons cooking oil
12–ounce can pineapple
   pieces
5-ounce carton soured cream
1 chicken stock cube
$\frac{1}{4}$ pint boiling water
2 teaspoons lemon juice
2 tablespoons vinegar
1 level tablespoon cornflour
1 ounce flaked almonds
   (toasted)

FRY THE CHICKEN drumsticks in the oil until golden
brown on all sides. Drain the pineapple cubes and stir
the pineapple into the pan with the soured cream.
Dissolve the stock cube in the boiling water, stir in the
pineapple juice, lemon juice, vinegar and cornflour.
Pour this mixture into the pan over the chicken and
bring to the boil, stirring. Reduce the heat to simmering
and cook the chicken for 1 hour. To serve, turn into a
serving dish and sprinkle with the almonds.
Serves 8

Chocolate Fondue

8 ounces plain chocolate
2 tablespoons warm water
1 eating apple (sliced)
1 orange (segmented)
1 large banana (sliced)
10–ounce can pineapple
   pieces
1 eating pear (cubed)

PUT THE CHOCOLATE into a small pan. Add the water
and heat very gently until the chocolate melts. Stir in
more water if necessary to make a sauce which will
thickly coat the back of a wooden spoon. Transfer the
pot to a fondue burner on the table.
   Put the various fruits on individual dishes and let each
person spear fruit and dip it in the chocolate sauce.
Serves 8

Beans and Bangers Cauldron

2 20-ounce tins baked beans
2 pounds beef sausagemeat
2 large onions (chopped)
2 large eggs (beaten)
salt and pepper
Worcester sauce
plain flour
1 ounce dripping

TURN THE BEANS into a huge saucepan. Mix the sausagemeat with the onions, eggs, salt, pepper and Worcester sauce to season. Form the mixture into 1-inch diameter balls, flouring your hands as they become sticky. Melt the dripping in a large frying-pan and fry the balls until they are golden brown and cooked right through.

Meanwhile, heat the baked beans. When hot, drain the sausagemeat balls and stir them into the cauldron. Leave on a hot tray to keep hot throughout the evening.
Serves 8

Fruit in the Pan

4 large bananas
8-ounce can pineapple rings
1 tablespoon lemon juice
  (strained)
2 ounces Demerara sugar
1 level teaspoon ground mace
2 ounces butter

PEEL AND SLICE the bananas lengthways. Drain the pineapple rings but save the juice. Cover the bananas with the lemon juice, then add the pineapple rings and sprinkle with the sugar and mace. Heat the butter in a very heavy frying-pan. Add the fruit and lemon juice mixture. Pour on the pineapple syrup and bring to the boil. Let the fruit simmer until the bananas are soft but not soggy.
Serves 8

Herb-Baked Bread

1 French loaf
6 ounces butter
2 level teaspoons mixed
  dried herbs

PREPARE AS FOR garlic bread (see page 68) but beat herbs into the butter and use to spread in the slices. Bake for about 15 minutes at Gas 6/400°F.
Serves 8

Tomato Sauce

1 small onion (chopped)
1 small carrot (chopped)
1 ounce butter
½ ounce cornflour
1 pound soft ripe tomatoes
  (chopped)
1 level dessertspoon tomato
  purée
1 chicken stock cube
½ pint boiling water
salt and pepper
1 level teaspoon dried
  marjoram

FRY THE ONION and carrot in the butter in a large saucepan for about 5 minutes. Stir in the cornflour, tomatoes and tomato purée. Dissolve the stock cube in the boiling water and pour into the pan with salt and pepper, marjoram, bay leaf and sugar. Stir and bring to the boil. Simmer for about 45 minutes or until the vegetables are cooked. Sieve or blend the contents of the pan and return to a rinsed saucepan to reheat. Check seasoning and serve hot with sausages.
Serves 4–6

1 bay leaf
1 level teaspoon caster sugar

Apricot Velvet

1 packet lemon jelly
¼ pint double cream
8-ounce can apricot halves
1 ounce flaked almonds
  (toasted)

MAKE UP THE packet jelly according to the directions on the packet but use ¼ pint less water than stated. Whisk the jelly. Whisk the cream lightly and whisk into the jelly. Strain the apricots and chop the fruit. Stir into the jelly and pour into glasses and leave to set. Decorate with flaked almonds to serve.
Serves 6

Chicken Puffs

1 pound chicken (cooked)
2 ounces butter
4 ounces onion (chopped)
2 ounces plain flour
½ pint milk
salt and pepper
lemon juice (strained)
13-ounce packet frozen puff
  pastry

CUT THE CHICKEN into small pieces. Melt the butter in a large pan. Fry the onion for 5 minutes until soft and just beginning to colour. Stir in the flour, cook for 2 minutes, stirring all the time. Remove from the heat and stir in the milk. Season with salt and pepper and return to the heat. Bring to the boil and cook, stirring for 3 minutes. Stir in lemon juice to taste and the chicken pieces and leave to cool.

Allow the pastry to thaw at room temperature for at least 1 hour if still frozen. Roll out on a lightly floured board to a ¼-inch thickness. Cut out 24 4-inch rounds using a plain cutter. Put a spoonful of chicken filling in the centre of each round, moisten the edge of the pastry with water and fold over to make a half-moon shape. Press the edges well to seal. Arrange on damp baking sheets and bake for about 20 minutes at Gas 8/450°F. Serve hot. If liked, cook beforehand and reheat at Gas 4/350°F. for about 15 minutes.
Makes 24

Pineapple and Banana Fritters

4 ounces plain flour
pinch salt
2 tablespoons vegetable oil
¼ pint tepid water
6 large bananas (peeled)
1 large egg white (whisked)
oil or fat for deep frying
caster sugar
15-ounce can pineapple rings
  (drained)

SIFT THE FLOUR and salt into a bowl. Make a well in the centre. Add the oil and mix to a batter with the tepid water. Cover and leave to stand for 30 minutes. Cut the bananas in half lengthways. Fold the egg white into the batter and dip in the banana halves. Deep fry for about 6 minutes, then drain well and toss in caster sugar. Dry the pineapple well on kitchen paper, coat with the remaining batter and deep fry for about 8 minutes. Drain and toss in caster sugar.
Serves 8

Open Sandwiches

24 slices bread (white,
brown, granary, wheatgerm)
10 ounces butter (softened)
12 lettuce leaves (washed)
2 slices liver pâté
2 small chicken joints
(cooked)
2 large slices beef (cooked)
2 large slices pork (cooked)
2 large slices lamb (cooked)
6 thin slices luncheon meat
3 hard-boiled eggs (sliced)
8 slices salami
3 ounces shrimps (peeled)
6 ounces blue cheese
1 crumbed plaice fillet (fried)
4 slices ham (cooked)
2 large pickled onions
4 rashers streaky bacon
(crisply fried)
2 bacon rolls (fried)
2 large tomatoes (sliced)
2 gherkin fans (see page 55)
1 gherkin (finely chopped)
6 level tablespoons
mayonnaise (see page 19)
1 level tablespoon parsley
(finely chopped)
2 level tablespoons
horseradish sauce
1 large lemon (sliced)
2-inch piece cucumber
(sliced)
parsley sprigs
watercress sprigs
2 level tablespoons chives
(snipped)
1 small onion (sliced)
4 black grapes (halved)
2 heaped tablespoons
Russian salad
1 heaped tablespoon pickled
red cabbage

SPREAD THE BREAD generously with butter and arrange lettuce leaves on 8 slices. Tear the other lettuce leaves into pieces for garnish. Put pâté on 2 plain slices and chicken on 2 lettuce-covered slices. Arrange the beef, pork, lamb and luncheon meat on another 8 slices of bread. Put egg slices from 2 hard-boiled eggs on lettuce-covered slices. Fold the salami and arrange on 2 bread slices; and the shrimps on another 2 slices of bread. The cheese should be arranged on lettuce. Cut the plaice fillet in half and put on the 2 remaining lettuce-covered slices. Arrange the ham on the last 2 plain bread slices.

Cut the pickled onions in half and arrange on the roast lamb. Put 2 bacon rashers diagonally across the liver pâté and 2 more down the length of the egg sandwiches. Put the bacon rolls with the roast chicken.

Arrange tomato slices on the roast lamb. Add a gherkin fan to the roast beef. Stir the chopped gherkin into 2 tablespoons mayonnaise. Spoon on to the plaice sandwiches. Add slices of egg. Put a spoonful of mayonnaise in the middle of the hard-boiled egg sandwiches and down the centre of the shrimps. Sprinkle parsley on the lamb and serve. Add a tomato twist to the liver pâté, sprinkle with parsley and serve. Spoon horseradish on to the beef sandwiches. Top the shrimps with lemon slice twists. Add cucumber slices to the roast pork. Garnish the beef with parsley sprigs and serve. Add watercress to the roast pork. Sprinkle the egg sandwiches with chives and also the plaice sandwiches; serve both. Separate the onion slices into rings and garnish the salami sandwiches and ham sandwiches. Add a piece of lettuce to each and a tomato twist to the ham and serve. Arrange the grapes on the cheese and serve. Spoon the Russian salad on to the luncheon meat, add tomato and cucumber slices and watercress sprigs and serve. Spoon the red cabbage on to the pork and serve. Garnish the chicken with watercress sprigs and serve. Add parsley sprigs to the shrimps and serve.

Serves 24

Apricot Crisp Triangles

4 ounces butter
4 level tablespoons golden
  syrup
4 ounces icing sugar (sifted)
6 ounces cornflakes (slightly
  crushed)
15-ounce can apricot halves
glacé cherries
angelica leaves
5-ounce carton double cream
1 level teaspoon arrowroot

MELT THE BUTTER and golden syrup in a large pan. Stir in the icing sugar and cornflakes and stir to mix well. Divide the mixture between 2 8-inch sandwich tins which should be greased. Press the mixture down well and smooth the top. Mark into 6 portions in each tin. Leave to set in the fridge for about 2 hours. When set, just warm the base of each tin to loosen the crisp. Cut each one into 6 triangles. Drain the apricots. Cut each glacé cherry in half. Cut the angelica into diamond shapes to look like leaves. Whisk the cream until thick. Spread a little on each triangle and arrange an apricot half, cut side up at the wide end of each triangle. Put the remaining cream in a piping bag fitted with a large star nozzle. Pipe stars of cream in each apricot and top with a cherry half. Pipe a star at each point and decorate with angelica. Blend the arrowroot with a little cold water. Heat the apricot juice and pour on to the arrowroot. Return to the pan, bring to the boil and stir all the time while you cook the sauce for 2 minutes. It should be thick and clear. Serve separately in a jug.
Serves 12

Piquant Dip

15-ounce can pineapple
  pieces
5-ounce carton cream cheese
1 heaped tablespoon salad
  cream
1 level tablespoon brown
  chutney
lemon juice (strained)

STRAIN THE PINEAPPLE and push a cocktail stick into each piece. Arrange them on a plate. Beat the cream cheese with the salad cream and chutney. Thin to a dipping consistency with the pineapple juice and a little lemon juice. Serve in a small bowl in the middle of the plate.

Pineapple Dip

8 ounces cottage cheese
5-ounce carton soured cream
salt and pepper
8-ounce can pineapple
  tidbits
1 level dessertspoon chives
  (snipped)
crisps

MIX THE COTTAGE cheese and soured cream with salt and pepper to season. Drain the pineapple and stir the pieces into the dip. Stir in the chives and spoon into a small dish. Surround with the crisps or with small savoury biscuits and serve.

Petits Fours (page 104). Overleaf,
Wedding Cake (page 106)

Iced Orange Tea

1 pint strong cold black tea
crushed ice
1–2 ounces caster sugar
juice of 1 orange (strained)
1 large orange (thinly sliced)
sprigs of mint or lemon thyme

POUR THE TEA over the crushed ice and stir in the sugar to taste. Chill in the fridge, then add the juice of the orange. Serve decorated with orange slices and mint or lemon thyme sprigs.
Serves 6

Brazilian Chocolate

4 ounces plain chocolate
½ pint strong black hot coffee
2 pints milk

MELT THE CHOCOLATE in a basin over a pan of hot water. Add the coffee and stir to mix. Heat, stirring all the time, for 1 minute. Heat the milk in a large saucepan. When almost boiling, stir in the chocolate and coffee mixture and whisk continuously until frothy on top and very hot, but not boiling. Pour into heatproof glasses or mugs and serve at once.
Serves 8

Fresh Fruit Cups

8 ounces plain chocolate
6 ounces sponge cake
4 tablespoons brandy
6 level tablespoons raspberry
conserve
8 ounces fresh or frozen
raspberries
5-ounce carton double cream
1 level teaspoon arrowroot

MELT THE CHOCOLATE in a small basin standing over a pan of hot water. Using a fairly thick paint brush and two paper cake cases together, coat the inside with chocolate. Leave to harden while you coat 11 more. Paint on another 2 or 3 coats until the chocolate is used. Leave to set completely. Crumble the sponge cake into fine crumbs. Stir in the brandy. Heat the conserve until runny, then sieve to remove the seeds. Pour half into the crumbs and mix together. When cool, spoon a little into each chocolate case, after easing each one carefully from its paper case. The easiest way is to tear off the cases. Allow frozen raspberries to thaw a little but not to become soft. Whip the cream and put into a piping bag fitted with a small star nozzle. Blend the arrowroot with a little cold water. Stir in a little of the remaining raspberry conserve and transfer with the rest of the conserve to a small pan. Bring to the boil, stirring while the sauce thickens and clears. Add a little hot water if the sauce is too thick. It should just coat the back of a wooden spoon. Fill the cases with fruit, spoon on the glaze and pipe cream around the cases. Serve at once.
Makes 12

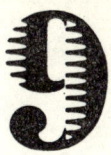

Celebration Parties

CELEBRATION PARTIES ARE usually the occasion for a special cake, which often provides the table's centrepiece. Into this category come the wedding breakfast, christening and engagement party, silver wedding party, twenty-first (or eighteenth) birthday party or any other birthday party and just-achieved-something parties like passing exams or a driving test.

For weddings, there is an impressive range of paperware for the table in traditional white and silver. If the cake is displayed on its own for the convenience of those wishing to photograph the cake-cutting ceremony, a stunning centrepiece becomes essential, and to this end it is worth considering the white, silver and blue 'towers' of wedding bells available from paper tableware stockists. Making the cake can be a great problem for those who don't make many cakes or who aren't nimble-fingered with decorating utensils. Don't attempt anything fancy. If you want to make your own wedding cake, think of it in terms of just one tier and make one cake at a time, then it won't seem like an endless task. Ask for help with the flat icing if you know someone who's skilled with royal icing. It's a tricky job, but the second coat will give you heart. It always looks marvellous, even though it doesn't seem possible that anything can be made of a very dodgy first coat. And it's always possible to use a very fine sandpaper to smooth out imperfections on each coat of flat icing. The final flowing coat which covers the whole cake and the board can be repeated twice for a perfectly smooth and ultra-professional finish. So don't be worried that you have to repeat coats. This is exactly how the professional cake-makers achieve a perfect finish. Practise piping on sponge cakes beforehand keeping the decoration simple like stars and shells if this is your first go at piping. You can always add to the piping with silver balls, with bought horseshoes, bows, bells, slippers, sugar rosebuds, mimosa balls and so on, using the icing more as a kind of glue than the decoration itself. Use ribbons a lot, making them into tiny bows to cover the weak spots in your flat icing. The most suitable type is satin paper ribbon, the kind which sticks when moistened. Make streamers which can reach from the top tier to the bottom, first splitting the ribbon into narrow widths, curling it and then letting it fall, securing it to the tiers in places with a little icing. Use fresh

4

flowers to crown the whole cake, or rice paper flowers which you can find in some stationers' shops. Or make them out of almond paste coloured with vegetable colourings to the right shades for the flower petals.

Cakes for a christening are often the top tiers of wedding cakes and if you're thinking of saving the top tier of your wedding cake, remove the icing before you store it. Mould can grow between the almond paste and the royal icing and spoil the whole cake without you knowing about it. If you keep the tier for a year you'll have to re-ice it anyway because the icing discolours, so you lose nothing by taking the icing off straight away.

If you haven't saved the top tier of your wedding cake, make a rich but plain cake for the christening. There will probably be more children about than for any other party, particularly as christenings are popularly held in the afternoon, to be followed by a tea. The cake given in this chapter can be almond iced and then royal iced and decorated as you like. Sugared almonds make a pretty and unusual decoration (in Greece, they're thrown at weddings to signify the wish that the couple be blessed with lots of children). You could decorate a wedding cake with them for a difference though I'd keep quiet about the significance of the decoration.

Silver wedding cakes can be either rich fruit cakes, simple sponge cakes or the rich sponge cake mixture. You could always decorate it with a small piece of real silver, which could be your present to the couple. Bought silver leaves, bells and bows can be used here, though silver ribbons, the kind used for tying Christmas parcels, would be more effective and less usual. Form it into a large pompom bow and secure it to the centre of the cake with streamers coming from the pompom over the sides of the cake to the board, secured at each place with an icing star.

For most other celebrations, it's enough to hold a party without going to the trouble of making a cake with a car key and a driving licence, or a mortar board and scroll motif on the top—though these things are a marvellous challenge if you're used to making novelty cakes. I'd use almond paste for this kind of decoration, drawing them out first on paper and then cutting out patterns to use as a template when cutting the decorations themselves. Almond paste colours well so don't forget to use the vegetable colours to achieve different effects.

How you set the table is perhaps the most important part of a celebration party. It's the time to use your best cloth and napkins crisply starched or to show off your skills by folding paper napkins into any one of the fancy shapes shown with step-by-step illustrations on pages 11–12. The buffet fold is my particular favourite because setting out dozens of knives and forks is always a problem. They take up so much space and it's not easy to make them look decorative. Each napkin folded into the buffet fold can hold the cutlery in the pocket.

Try to decorate the tablecloth itself, especially if it's a plain white one. I've tacked artificial flowers around the edge for a party, using two colours to echo the colour scheme of the plates. Plain white, or white and silver, or white and pink could be used for a wedding or christening, and gayer colours for other celebration parties. You could also cut doilies in half to form semi-circles and tack or stick these in place around the edge of the table—straight edges to the edge to form a scallop decoration. Use plain white ones, silver or gold.

Flower arrangements for special parties can be a little more elaborate than those you would do for a dinner party. Try a long low arrangement almost the length of the table or lots of small bunches here and there. You could also tuck a single flower into each napkin or make a posy for each person using a single flower and a silver, gold or white doily gathered round the outside. It may be necessary to cut out the centres of the larger doilies to get a particularly pretty effect, especially when you want to cover small plates and don't have small enough doilies.

Other centrepieces which are very effective are bought paper ones such as wedding bells and Easter bunnies, which with very little effort transform a plain table into a pretty one. You can see a wedding bells centrepiece in the photograph of the wedding cake opposite page 97.

You can plan the party as a buffet or as a sit-down meal. It depends largely on the space you've got, the number of guests, whether or not it's summer and you can eat in the garden or whether it is to be rather formal with speeches and toasts.

Though champagne is the traditional drink for weddings, christenings, engagements and twenty-first birthday parties, the price is so high nowadays that a sparkling white wine is often served instead. You may like to serve a cheap wine throughout the party, opening one or two bottles of champagne for the toasts and the speeches.

Invitations for the more formal kind of celebration party should be formal and for weddings are usually printed. For christenings, if it's just the family, then word of mouth is enough, but if you are inviting lots of people, then it's worth having the invitations printed. Silver and golden wedding celebrations may be family occasions or more formal, especially in the case of the golden wedding.

Family parties deserve a word here. They would seem to be the easiest type of party because everyone knows everyone and you'd think you could be completely relaxed. However, in some ways they're one of the most difficult kinds of party. Guests will range from toddlers to grannies and all the generations in between. I think it's impossible to keep everyone happy all the time when ages, tastes and desires are so disparate. You will obviously provide a range of food that's suitable for everyone from the babies to Grandma, but it's worth giving a little more thought to each individual. Perhaps you could include something in the occasion that will please everyone—a colouring book to keep a toddler quiet, while Granny would appreciate a small present of some luxury that her pension won't run to. Many a young housewife with a family to feed won't have money to treat herself to (say) a tin of salmon, so a salmon mousse (made economically with pink salmon, white sauce and other seasonings) would go down well. Let the men go off to the pub for a pint half way through the evening if they wish, especially if they're going to be impossible if they stay at home.

Serve something deliciously savoury with coffee towards the end of the evening —something like cheese twists, which can be made a couple of days in advance and heated through in the oven while you make the coffee. Or provide little biscuits or cakes with a hot chocolate drink, made special with a dollop of cream on top, or with marshmallows sprinkled with cinnamon and left to melt gradually.

Lemon Sorbet

8 ounces sugar lumps
1 pint water
3 large lemons
2 large egg whites

PUT THE SUGAR and water in a saucepan and heat gently, stirring until dissolved, then bring to the boil and boil for about 8 minutes or until syrupy.

Finely grate the rind from the lemons and squeeze out and strain the juice. Stir rind and juice into the syrup and mix well. Turn the mixture into an ice-making tray and put in the ice-making compartment of your fridge or into the freezer. Freeze for about 1½ hours or until half-frozen. Whisk the egg whites until stiff. Remove the ice, whisk it thoroughly, fold in the egg whites and return mixture to freezer to freeze until solid.
Serves 4

Roast Ribs with Yorkshire Pudding

7-pound piece foreribs of beef
2 ounces dripping
4 ounces plain flour
pinch salt
1 large egg
¼ pint milk
¼ pint cold water

PUT THE MEAT in a roasting tin and add the dripping. Roast the meat (15 minutes per pound) at Gas 8/450°F., reducing the heat to Gas 6/400°F. after the first 30 minutes' cooking. Sift the flour and salt into a basin. Make a well in the centre, drop in the egg and mix to a smooth batter with the milk and water. Beat the batter well, then leave it to stand for 30 minutes. Three-quarters of an hour before the meat is ready, put a teaspoon of fat from the meat tin in each of 12 patty tins. Put the tins in the oven above the meat to become really hot. Pour in the batter and cook the puddings for about 35 minutes or until well risen and golden.
Serves 12

Salmon Brandade

1½ pounds fresh salmon
2 parsley stalks
juice of 1 lemon (strained)
salt and pepper
1 small carrot (peeled)
1 small onion (skinned)
1 bay leaf

WIPE THE SALMON and put it in a saucepan. Add the parsley, ½ the lemon juice, pinch of salt, carrot, onion, bay leaf and thyme. Pour on 2 pints cold water. Bring to the boil slowly, then when boiling, reduce the heat and simmer for 20 minutes or until the fish will flake easily. Remove from the pan and flake, discarding skin and bones.

1 sprig thyme
1 garlic clove (crushed)
¼ pint olive oil
6 tablespoons double cream
croûtons (see page 27) made
    into triangles

Put the fish into a blender with the garlic, 5 table-spoons olive oil and 3 tablespoons cream. Blend, adding the remaining oil and cream very gradually until they are incorporated into a completely smooth mixture. Turn the mixture into the top of a double saucepan and simmer gently for 10 minutes. Stir in the remaining lemon juice and season with salt and black pepper, freshly ground if possible. Serve with croûtons made in the shape of triangles.

If the brandade is to be served cold, serve it with toast fingers.

Serves 6

Irish Coffee

8 sugar lumps
8 tablespoons Irish whiskey
1 pint strong black hot coffee
½ pint double cream

PUT 2 SUGAR lumps in each of 4 wine glasses. Add 2 tablespoons Irish whiskey to each glass. Pour on the coffee and stir to dissolve the sugar. Gently pour the cream on top of each glass. There is no need to pour it over the back of a spoon, provided the Irish coffee has been sweetened.

Serves 4

Spinach Quiches

8 ounces plain flour
pinch salt
2 ounces margarine
2 ounces lard
2 pounds spinach
2 ounces butter
¼ pint double cream
ground nutmeg
pepper
croûtons (see page 27)

SIFT THE FLOUR and salt into a bowl. Rub in the margarine and lard and mix to a stiff dough with cold water. Roll on a lightly floured board and use to line 4 4-inch fluted flan tins or tartlet tins. Fill with greaseproof paper and baking beans and bake blind for 10 minutes at Gas 6/400°F., then remove beans and paper and bake for another 5 minutes or until golden brown and crisp.

Wash the spinach in lots of changes of water, discarding damaged leaves and thick ribs. Cook in the water clinging to the leaves for about 5 minutes. Drain well and blend the spinach with the butter, cream and nutmeg. Turn into a saucepan and stir the spinach to heat thoroughly. Season with salt and freshly ground black pepper and more nutmeg if necessary. Should the purée be too soft to be used in the tartlets, cook stirring over a fairly high heat until some of the excess water is driven off. Spoon the spinach into the tartlet tins and garnish with tiny croûtons.

Serves 4

Chocolate Mousse

6 ounces plain chocolate
2 tablespoons cold water
2 tablespoons orange Curaçao
4 large eggs (separated)
grated chocolate

BREAK THE CHOCOLATE into a basin with the water. Stand the basin over a pan of hot water and let the chocolate melt. Remove from the heat and allow to cool a little. Stir in the orange Curaçao and the egg yolks. Whisk the egg whites until stiff, but not dry and gently fold them into the chocolate mixture. Turn into individual dishes and leave to set. Chill before serving. Decorate with grated chocolate.
Serves 6

Pancakes with Apricots

4 ounces plain flour
pinch salt
1 large egg
½ pint milk
2 ounces lard
8-ounce can apricots
2 ounces butter
1 ounce almond nibs
   (toasted)
1 level teaspoon ground
   cinnamon

SIFT THE FLOUR and salt into a bowl. Make a well in the centre; drop in the egg and mix to a smooth batter with the milk. Fry 8 thin large pancakes using about ¼ ounce lard to grease the frying-pan each time. Layer the pancakes with foil on a plate standing over a pan of hot water to keep them hot and moist.

Strain the apricots, reserving the juice. Purée the fruit. Put it in a pan and heat gently, stirring frequently as moisture is driven off and the purée thickens. Melt the butter in a large frying-pan. Stir in the apricot syrup. Place a spoonful of apricot purée in the centre of each pancake and arrange them in the frying-pan in the syrup. Heat gently, spooning the syrup over the pancakes. Serve sprinkled with the almonds and cinnamon.
Serves 4–6

Haricots Verts au Gratin

1 pound haricots verts
salt and pepper
1 ounce butter
1 ounce plain flour
½ pint milk
3 ounces Cheddar cheese
   (grated)
1 ounce Parmesan cheese
   (grated)

TRIM THE BEANS, removing any strings if necessary. Cook in plenty of boiling salted water for about 20 minutes or until tender, but still a bit crisp. Meanwhile, melt the butter in a saucepan. Stir in the flour to make a roux. Gradually stir in the milk off the heat, then return to the heat and bring to the boil, stirring. Cook, stirring for 3 minutes. Stir in 2 ounces of Cheddar cheese and season well with salt and pepper.

Drain the beans and stir them into the sauce. Pour the mixture into an ovenproof dish. Sprinkle with the remaining Cheddar cheese and the Parmesan and grill under a hot grill until the top is brown and bubbly.
Serves 4

Peas with Onions

1 pound frozen peas
5-ounce packet frozen onions
　　in white sauce
mint (finely chopped) or
　　parsley (finely chopped)

COOK THE PEAS according to the directions on the packet. Cook the onions in white sauce according to their directions. Drain the peas well and stir them into the onions. Pour into a serving dish and preferably sprinkle with finely chopped mint, though parsley will do.
Serves 8

Courgettes Vinaigrette

2 pounds courgettes
salt
1 large onion (sliced)
vinaigrette (see page 19)
parsley (finely chopped)

CUT THE COURGETTES into 1-inch pieces, removing the stem and stalk ends. Cook in boiling salted water for about 10 minutes or until cooked and tender, but still a bit crisp. Drain well. Separate the onion slices into rings. Put the courgettes in a large bowl. Pour on the vinaigrette while still warm and toss well. Add the onion rings and parsley and serve chilled.
Serves 8

Spinach and Bacon Salad

1½ pounds really fresh
　　spinach (best taken straight
　　from the garden)
6 rashers streaky bacon
juice of 1 lemon (strained)
6 tablespoons salad oil
pepper

SORT THE SPINACH, discarding damaged leaves and remove the thick ribs. Wash the spinach well in several changes of water to remove grit. Drain well then dry in a tea-towel, gathering the corners and swinging the tea-towel round to remove the water without damaging the leaves. Arrange on another dry tea-towel and pat the leaves dry.

While you continue to dry the leaves, fry the bacon until it is crisp enough to crumble. (Don't remove the rinds; when crisp they are delicious in this salad.) Tear the spinach leaves into small pieces and put in a salad bowl. Sprinkle on the bacon pieces. Whisk the lemon juice and salad oil and season with plenty of freshly-ground black pepper. Pour over the salad, toss well and serve at once.
Serves 6

Potted Chicken

8 ounces chicken (cooked)
6 ounces ham (cooked)
salt and pepper
ground nutmeg
6 ounces unsalted butter

MINCE THE CHICKEN and ham finely and season with salt, pepper and nutmeg. Soften the butter and gradually work in 4 ounces to make a smooth paste. Press the paste into 8 small pots or into 1 large one. Chill until firm. Melt the remaining butter and pour it, after cooling a little, over the top of each pot. Leave to set in the fridge. Serve with toast.
Serves 8

Melba Toast

¼-inch thick slices of white bread

TOAST THE BREAD on both sides to golden brown, then carefully split each slice. Toast the uncooked sides gently until crisp.

Petits Fours

Almond Petits Fours:
2 large egg whites
6 ounces ground almonds
3 ounces caster sugar
almond essence
glacé cherries
angelica

WHISK THE EGG whites until stiff, then fold in the ground almonds, sugar and a few drops almond essence. Turn the mixture into a piping bag fitted with a large star nozzle. Pipe stars, fingers, circles and whirls on to a baking sheet covered with rice paper or with silicone or other non-stick paper. Decorate each biscuit with a small piece of glacé cherry or angelica. Bake for about 15 minutes or until they are just beginning to turn golden brown at Gas 2/300°F. Remove with a palette knife and cool on a wire rack.
Makes 20

Marzipan Fruits:
4 ounces icing sugar
1 large egg yolk
6 ounces ground almonds
vegetable colourings such as brown, red, green and yellow
angelica
cloves

SIFT THE ICING sugar into a large bowl. Add the egg yolk. Whisk the mixture over a pan of hot water until the mixture is thick enough to hold a trail from the whisk. Work in the ground almonds then knead to a paste. Add a little more sugar and ground almonds if it is still too moist. Divide the mixture for apples, oranges, lemons and bananas. Colour the first part orange using a mixture of red and yellow, the second fairly deep yellow by mixing a little brown into the yellow. Colour the third part green and the fourth part yellow. Form the orange into round shapes and press each one against the smallest side of your grater to resemble orange peel. Push a clove in each one but remove the clove seed first. Form the deep yellow mixture into banana shapes and using a fine paint brush and the brown colouring lightly brush brown down the length to produce streaks which look like the natural markings of a ripe banana. Form the green marzipan into apple shapes and using the paint brush, brush on red for the rosy colouring. Stick a small piece of angelica in to form the stalk. Finally shape the yellow into lemons and press each one against the grater to form the peel.

This mixture can also be made into little vegetables. Potatoes should be coloured brown, shaped and then dusted with cocoa. Carrots should be bright orange with an angelica stalk. Turnips and swedes should also be given angelica stalks. Tomatoes should be red with

angelica stalks. Courgettes should be green with darker green stripes brushed along the length.
Makes 20

Truffles:
4½ ounces plain chocolate
4 tablespoons double cream
1 dessertspoon pink
  aromatic bitters
3 ounces cocoa
4 ounces icing sugar
chocolate vermicelli

MELT THE CHOCOLATE in a small bowl over a pan of hot water. Cool. Whip the cream until stiff, fold in the chocolate and bitters and leave until cold. Sift together 2 ounces cocoa and the icing sugar and beat it into the chocolate mixture. Shape into small balls and roll half in cocoa, and half in chocolate vermicelli. Put in sweet paper cases.
Makes 20

AFTER-DINNER MINTS (see page 36) can also be included in this section. If liked you can colour and flavour the mixture in different ways. Instead of the green colouring and peppermint flavouring, try yellow colouring and lemon essence, pink colouring and almond essence, or pale blue with vanilla essence.

Grilled Cutlets with Mushroom Sauce

8 lamb cutlets
1 medium onion (chopped)
1 medium carrot (chopped)
1 ounce dripping
1 ounce plain flour
½ pint brown stock
salt and pepper
2 ounces button mushrooms
  (chopped)
cutlet frills

ASK YOUR BUTCHER to prepare the cutlets by cutting away 1 inch of fat and meat, leaving the bone scraped clean. Fry the onion and carrot in the dripping in a heavy based saucepan. Cook for about 10 minutes, then stir in the flour and cook the mixture very very gently for about 20 minutes or until it is a rich brown colour. The mixture is very likely to catch on the bottom at this stage, and if it does it will give the sauce a bitter taste. If it does catch, but only slightly, complete the sauce and make up the colour with a spot of gravy browning. Gradually stir in the stock off the heat, then return the sauce to the heat and bring to the boil, stirring all the time. Cover the pan and simmer the sauce gently for 20 minutes. Season the sauce with salt and pepper and add the mushrooms and simmer the sauce for another 10 minutes.

Grill the cutlets during this last 10 minutes' cooking time, turning them frequently. Arrange on a serving plate, add a cutlet frill to each cutlet bone and serve the sauce separately.
Serves 4

Potatoes Amandine

1 pound cooked potatoes
  (mashed)
3 large egg yolks (beaten)
salt and pepper
plain flour
1 large egg (beaten)
3 ounces flaked almonds
oil or fat for deep frying

MIX THE POTATOES with the egg yolks and salt and pepper to season. The mixture should be fairly dry. Form the mixture into balls. Season a little plain flour with salt and pepper. Coat the balls first in seasoned flour, then in egg and finally in almonds, pressing them on well. Fry in deep oil or fat until golden brown. Drain on kitchen paper and serve at once.
Serves 4

Quick Brown Rolls

1-pound packet brown soda
  bread mix
2 ounces margarine
½ pint water
plain flour

EMPTY THE CONTENTS of the packet into a bowl. Rub in the margarine and make a well in the centre. Add all the water and mix to a soft dough. Sprinkle with a little flour, knead lightly and form into 15 rolls. Arrange on greased baking sheets and bake for 25 minutes or until golden brown at Gas 7/425°F.
Makes 15

Trout with Almonds and Cream

4 trout
2 large lemons
1 level tablespoon parsley
  (finely chopped)
salt and pepper
¼ pint single cream
4 ounces flaked almonds
  (toasted)
thin cucumber slices

ASK YOUR FISHMONGER to clean the trout but to leave on the heads and tails. Rinse the fish and arrange them in an oblong ovenproof dish. Peel off the rind from 1 lemon, cutting away all the bitter pith. Squeeze and strain the juice from both lemons. Pour the lemon juice over the fish. Add the rind and sprinkle with the parsley and salt and pepper. Add 2 tablespoons cold water and cover the dish. Bake for about 10 minutes at Gas 4/350°F.

Gently heat the cream. Pour over the fish and sprinkle with the almonds. Garnish with cucumber slices.
Serves 4

Wedding Cake

10-inch round cake:
1¼ pounds sultanas
1 pound currants
1 pound 2 ounces stoned
  raisins
8 ounces glacé cherries
6 ounces chopped mixed peel
4 ounces almond nibs
1¼ pounds plain flour

MAKE BOTH CAKES in exactly the same way. Mix the sultanas, currants and stoned raisins. Chop the cherries and add to the fruit with the mixed peel and almond nibs. Sift the flour with the cinnamon and nutmeg. Cream the butter and sugar until light in colour and very fluffy. Beat in the eggs gradually, beating well after each addition, then alternately fold in the sifted flour mixture and the dried fruits. Finally add the brandy, which should give you a very stiff dropping consistency. Spoon the

2 level teaspoons ground
cinnamon
1 level teaspoon ground
nutmeg
1 pound 2 ounces butter
1 pound 2 ounces soft brown
sugar
9 large eggs (beaten)
3 tablespoons brandy

7-inch round cake:
8 ounces sultanas
6 ounces currants
7 ounces stoned raisins
3 ounces glacé cherries
2 ounces chopped mixed peel
2 ounces almond nibs
8 ounces plain flour
½ level teaspoon ground
cinnamon
pinch ground nutmeg
6 ounces butter
6 ounces soft brown sugar
3 large eggs (beaten)
1 tablespoon brandy

Almond paste (1) *for the
10-inch cake:*
8 ounces icing sugar (sifted)
8 ounces caster sugar
1 pound ground almonds
1 teaspoon lemon juice
(strained)
2 large eggs (beaten)
1 pound apricot jam

(2) *for the 7-inch cake:*
4 ounces icing sugar (sifted)
4 ounces caster sugar
8 ounces ground almonds
few drops lemon juice
(strained)
1 large egg (beaten)
8 ounces apricot jam

mixture into the tins, which should be greased and double-lined with greaseproof paper. The paper should also be greased. Level the mixture, then hollow the centre so that it will bake flat. If it is more convenient, the cakes can be left overnight and baked the following day. Cover with a cloth and leave in a cool place.

Bake the 10-inch cake for about 6 hours and the 7-inch cake for about 3 hours at Gas 2/300°F.

Should either cake brown too much, turn the oven down to Gas 1/275°F. and cover the top with a double thickness of greaseproof paper, laying it on the lining papers rather than on top of the cake itself. It's a wise precaution to wrap these large cakes in two layers of brown paper securely tied with string before you bake them. Stand each tin on several thicknesses of paper. The deep colour of these rich cakes comes from the long slow baking.

MAKE THE ALMOND paste by mixing the icing and caster sugars in a large bowl. Stir in the ground almonds and mix to a smooth, firm paste with the lemon juice and beaten egg. Knead the paste lightly. It should be dry. Kneading a little will make it smoother but if your hands are very warm, you may find the almond paste is becoming too oily with the kneading. The oil could spoil the subsequent coating of royal icing.

Roll two-thirds of the almond paste, on a board lightly sprinkled with caster sugar, to a strip as wide as the cake is high and long enough to go right round. Heat the jam until it is runny, then sieve. Brush the sides of the cake with jam, then roll up the almond paste strip like a Swiss roll. Hold one short edge against the cake then unroll the strip round the cake pressing it lightly as you go. Join the cut edges smoothly and roll a jam jar around the sides to smooth out any finger marks. Brush the top of the cake with jam. Roll the remaining third of almond paste to a circle to fit the top of the cake. Put in position, join the edges smoothly and make them square by rolling the jam jar around again. Cover with greaseproof paper and leave for 2 weeks to dry out.

Royal icing (1) for the
10-inch cake:
2 pounds icing sugar (sifted)
4 large egg whites (lightly
    beaten)
1 teaspoon lemon juice
2 teaspoons glycerine

(2) for the 7-inch cake:
1 pound icing sugar (sifted)
2 large egg whites (lightly
    beaten)
1 teaspoon lemon juice
1 teaspoon glycerine

BEAT THE ICING sugar into the frothy egg whites until half has been added. Then stir in the lemon juice. Continue beating in the sugar until the mixture is white and stiff and glossy. This may take 10 to 15 minutes of beating. Beat in the glycerine. The mixture should hold a soft peak when pulled with a wooden spoon.

Keep the bowl of icing covered with a wet tea-towel during use. It is easier to apply the coatings to the top and sides on two separate days. Use a turn-table when adding royal icing. It makes it easy to get a good finish. Put a large quantity of icing on the top of the cake using a large palette knife. Spread it over the surface, making long figure-of-eight movements to smooth the icing and remove any air bubbles at the same time. Remove excess icing, then using a long straight flexible ruler or an icing ruler, draw it swiftly and smoothly across the top of the cake, taking excess icing with you and leaving a flat surface. (This isn't easy and you may have to have several goes at it.) Holding a clean palette knife by the side of the cake, rotate the cake to remove excess icing from the edge.

Cover the sides with icing, spreading it with the same movement used for the top. Holding the ruler or palette knife, rotate the cake against the blade, taking off excess icing and leaving a smooth flat surface. Leave to dry. You may find it necessary to smooth off bumps with fine sandpaper. Cover the cake top and sides with a second coat of slightly thinner icing which will be much easier and look much better than the first coat. Smooth with sandpaper again if necessary. To give an even smoother finish, thin the remaining icing to a flowing consistency with a little water. Stick each cake to a silver board, 2 inches larger than the cake itself, with a dab of royal icing. The icing should coat the back of the wooden spoon but flow smoothly. Pour the icing over the top of the cake and let it flow all over the cake and the board. Stand by with a knife to swiftly help it along if it seems to be missing any parts of the sides of the cake. Remove surplus icing from the edges of the board and leave to dry.

Decorating the cake:
Make up a quantity of royal icing as above but make it stiffer than for flat icing. The icing should hold a stiff peak for piping. Put the icing into a piping bag fitted with the appropriate nozzle. Pipe a border around the edge of the cake and silver board. Pipe along the top edge of the cake also. When dry, pipe round the edge of the board itself. The sides of the cake can be piped if

liked, using a writing nozzle to make loops of icing and smooth dots underneath like grapes.

Stick the pillars in place on the 10-inch tier using a little icing, making sure that it doesn't seep out underneath. Don't put the pillars in place until the icing is really dry and hard, otherwise they'll sink slightly and spoil the finished surface. Put the top layer in place to check the cake, though it is better not to leave it in place. Store the cakes separately and assemble on the day.

Decorate the cake with pink paper ribbon, tearing each strip into narrow lengths and curling each one by holding it over the cutting edge of scissors and quickly running the scissors to the end of the ribbon. Use small pink rosebuds, bought from the haberdashery department of a large store. Cut the stalks off the rosebuds and, using a dab of icing, position 2 rosebuds with a length of curled ribbon on the edge of the cake. Continue round the cake, positioning the rosebuds equally. Repeat with the top layer. Stick rosebuds and the ends of the ribbons to the sides of the cakes just above the piped borders. Use white and pink artificial flowers and silver leaves to make a small and delicate bouquet for the top of the cake.

You can also decorate with pleated ribbon, ironing on a stick-on finish at the back to make the ribbon firmer. Cut each end into points to finish. Use a small vase for the top and fill it with tiny fresh flowers such as lily-of-the-valley, miniature rosebuds, grape hyacinths, snowdrops and so on. Use a small arrangement of flowers to match the bride's bouquet. The florist will bind the stems so the flowers keep fresh and don't mark the cake.

It's possible to buy rice paper roses and other flowers which you can stick with icing all over the cake to form the sole decoration if you're unsure of your piping skills.

Christening Cake

10 ounces butter
10 ounces caster sugar
5 large eggs (beaten)
8 ounces plain flour
1½ level teaspoons baking powder
2 ounces ground almonds

CREAM THE BUTTER and sugar until light and fluffy. Beat in the eggs gradually, beating well after each addition. Sift the flour and baking powder with the ground almonds and fold into the creamed mixture. Turn into a greased and lined 9-inch round tin and smooth the top flat. Bake for about 2 hours at Gas 2/300°F. Leave to cool a little in the tin, then turn on to a wire rack to finish cooling.

Icing :
1¾ pounds almond paste
  (see page 107)
blue colouring or cochineal
2 pounds royal icing (see
  page 108)
narrow blue or pink ribbon

COVER THE CAKE with almond paste and royal icing as described for the wedding cake on pages 107–8. Colour the remaining royal icing either pale blue or pale pink and put it into a piping bag. Pipe decorations around the cake. Cut the ribbon into short lengths and tie in small bows. Secure each bow with a few stitches. Stick the bows to the cake with icing, putting them around the base of the cake where it joins the board, around the top edge and in a cluster in the centre or around a central stork decoration if liked. Leave to dry.

Silver Wedding Cake

10-inch rich fruit cake (see
  page 106)
  or 9-inch rich plain cake
  (see page 109)
silver leaves
silver horseshoes
white satin ribbon

STAND THE ICED cake on a silver cake board and if liked leave it plain. Using royal icing, stick silver leaves and horseshoes and other silver decorations in place. Tie a white satin ribbon round the cake and finish in a bow. Small silver bells make a pretty decoration tied to the bow of the ribbon. Top the cake with a small silver vase or container, filled with fresh flowers.

10

Occasional Parties

CHRISTMAS, NEW YEAR'S EVE, Easter, Hallowe'en and Guy Fawkes all have certain traditions without which the occasion wouldn't be the same. Christmas, the most important of these festivals, is celebrated without exception by almost everyone every year. The traditional foods are so much a part of our lives that there should be few major decisions to be taken about Christmas menus. Beyond making up one's mind between a turkey and a chicken or perhaps whether to try duck or goose this year, there shouldn't be much that's different from the year before. The Christmas pudding and cake should be made early as usual to give them time to mature, and the cake topped with a snowy white scene during the last week. You might try varying the traditional mince pies one year by making a few with a meringue topping instead of the usual second pastry crust, or by adding pastry stars, which make it easy to slip a little bit of brandy butter into each mince pie as they come out of the oven and before they reach the table—twice as delicious, and twice as fattening, I'm afraid.

Most of us will order a second piece of meat—the most popular being bacon or pork. It's very useful to have this joint in the larder ready for making late-night snacks, cocktail tit-bits, impromptu lunches, even a light Boxing Day lunch with a bit of salad rather than potatoes, sprouts, turkey and the sauces again.

Try making a lemon sorbet one year. It's a most refreshing sweet and actually has the property of settling a tum that's over-full. In olden days, sorbet was presented at banquets as a course on its own to act as a settler and to prepare the eaters for the next six courses.

No doubt you will want the table to look especially attractive on Christmas Day. A novel way of attracting attention to the centre of the table is to display one of the delightful Snowmen or Father Christmases, made in a form of honeycombed paper, which are now available in the shops. There are even place markers to match which help to brighten up the festive board.

New Year's Eve is celebrated more in the north than in the south, though in recent years the southerners, too, have very wisely begun to see out the old year and see in the new. Although there is no traditional New Year food to my knowledge

Sandwiches cut into fancy shapes
for a tea party (page 46) and a
selection of small cream cakes—
Eclairs (page 45), Palmiers
(page 46), Viennese Cookies
(page 47) and Brandy Snaps
(page 49). Make a Chocolate
Gâteau (page 48) your centrepiece

first-footing with a piece of coal is a very important tradition and so one needs to have enough food in the house to give the first-footers something besides the dram of whisky. A good hot home-made soup would be most welcome.

Easter and Mother's Day both fall in the spring when the weather is getting warmer and the spring flowers are just beginning to show in the gardens. Easter eggs are given on Easter morning and you can make your own chocolate eggs using moulds which are supplied by kitchen equipment shops. The two halves are stuck together with melted chocolate and you can pipe on decorations, either in more chocolate or using various icings in different colours: Easter chicks, bunnies, daffodils and other flowers, nests and eggs are among the seasonal motifs. Dyeing hard-boiled eggs is much easier and the children can help to do this, and also to decorate them afterwards. The vegetable colourings used for dyeing the shells are weak, and you require half a bottle of each to get a good colour in most cases. So rely on onion skins for the yellow, spinach or other greens for the green. Cochineal makes a good pink, and you'll have to buy blue colouring for the blue eggs. Plain-coloured eggs may be hidden around the house and garden for the children to hunt; you may like to supply them with written funny clues, too.

Decorating these coloured eggs is a simple job with a paintbrush and the children's paintbox. Or you could use a little glue and stick on braids and beads, silver balls and ribbons to make very fancy presents. Blown eggs are perhaps more suitable for this, particularly as these highly-decorated eggs can then be kept indefinitely. Put the egg point down in an egg rack or egg box and using a fine needle (the finest you can find) and a small hammer, tap, tap, tap a small hole in the top of the egg. Tap the needle through, don't push it because it's the pushing that cracks the shell. Once you've made a small hole, take a bigger needle and tap that through. Reverse the egg and tap a hole in the pointed end. Push a darning needle right through and wiggle it around inside the egg to break the yolk. Then blow through one hole and eventually all the egg will be forced out through the other hole. Clear and clean the egg by blowing a mouthful of clean water through the egg. Repeat until the water comes out clean. Then the egg can be painted and decorated with any type of material without fear that it will harm the egg inside.

Hot cross buns shouldn't be forgotten, and home-made ones are marvellous. Try this recipe. The only trouble with it is that you'll find yourself making up batches of two dozen day after day through the holiday. The Easter or simnel cake is a spicy rich fruit cake with almond paste on top but no icing. Eggs of marzipan can be formed to decorate the top, or you can add fluffy chicks and bunnies from stationers' shops. Special table decorations in the form of Easter bunnies can also be bought in the shops, and would be a delightful addition to a toddler's party.

Mother's Day used to be the occasion for simnel cake. When girls were in service

Fish Soufflé with Sauce
Mousseline (page 114)

this is the cake they were allowed to bake to take home to their mothers to show how well they were doing. I suppose it's because Easter Day and Mother's Day are so close that the simnel cake has now come to mean Easter to us. On Mother's Day, the children can make tea on their own and give mother a nice surprise—or as much of a surprise as their giggling, pointed comments and hints will allow, as they crash and bang in the kitchen (where you're definitely not allowed).

Hallowe'en is the day when the witches and hobgoblins are abroad. It's October 31 and the night before All Saints Day. Food should be spooky, in keeping with the occasion, and though there isn't much in the way of traditional food, the decoration and names can be appropriate: spider's web cakes, drinks called witch's brews, and chocolate cornflake mixtures made into balls and decorated, when hard, with pointed hats and faces made of glacé cherries. Black cat sponges should be glacé-iced with black icing and given whiskers and features of piped white icing.

Hollowed pumpkins should provide the Hallowe'en lighting. Put a candle in each one, having cut out eyes, nose and mouth so the light can come through. Use the pumpkin for a pie or for roasting round the Sunday joint. A traditional Hallowe'en game is bobbing for apples. Apples are floated on a tub of water and everyone has their hands tied behind them. The idea is to try to grab an apple with your teeth—not so easy without getting completely soaked, so perhaps this is a game for men only. Let the women try and peel an apple all in one go. The continuous curly peel signifies continuing true love. Next they must throw the peel over their left shoulder while thinking of their true love. The peel should fall in the initial of the man in their life. And if it's not the initial of their husband's name, let them talk their way out of that while you bring on some mulled wine.

Guy Fawkes night is bonfire night and firework night, and I think the little parties held in back gardens are far more fun than the more organised large parties. Provided there is always an adult about looking after children while the fireworks are lit, then I see nothing wrong in having these parties. Make the bonfire as big as possible. It's often very cold on bonfire night and sometimes it's damp, so you'll need the warmth. Roast chestnuts and bake potatoes in the ashes. Hand round great mugs of chocolate, or coffee laced with something stronger. Steaming mugs of soup will be welcome and so will simple but hearty grub like sausage rolls, pasties, pork pies and so on. Gingerbread is a traditional treat for this time of the year. Make it a sticky one, moist and gingery, rather than the sponge sort, which I find rather dry. Keep pets indoors, wrap children up tight, and you'll enjoy the evening too.

Fish Soufflé with Sauce Mousseline

1 ounce butter
1 ounce plain flour
¼ pint milk
3 large eggs (separated)
salt and pepper
3 ounces brill, haddock or
   salmon (flaked)

Mousseline sauce:
2 large egg yolks
2 teaspoons warm water
4 ounces unsalted butter
   (softened)
salt and pepper
lemon juice (strained)
2 tablespoons double cream
   (whipped)

MELT THE BUTTER in a saucepan. Stir in the flour and cook the mixture for 2 minutes. Gradually stir in the milk off the heat. Bring to the boil, stirring. Allow to cool. Whisk the egg whites until stiff. Stir the egg yolks, seasoning and fish into the mixture, then fold in the egg whites. Turn the mixture into a 7-inch greased soufflé dish and bake for about 35 minutes at Gas 6/400°F.

To make the mousseline sauce, whisk the egg yolks and warm water together in a double saucepan or use a basin standing over a pan of hot water, because this sauce must not boil. Very gradually add the softened butter, whisking all the time. When it has been incorporated, season the sauce with salt, pepper and lemon juice. Finally, gently whisk in the whipped cream and serve with the soufflé.
Serves 4

Gravy

2 tablespoons fat
1–2 ounces plain flour
stock

REMOVE THE ROAST to a serving dish and keep hot. Pour off the fat from the tin, leaving behind about 2 tablespoons fat and all the juices and bits of meat or poultry. Stir in 1 to 2 ounces of plain flour, depending on how thick you like your gravy. It should be thin for beef, thick for lamb and fairly thin for roast poultry. Cook the mixture gently over a low heat to give it a rich brown colour, though the meat deposits should give sufficient colour. Gradually add stock (giblet stock, bone stock or vegetable water) and bring to the boil. Reduce the heat and simmer for 15 minutes. Season with salt and pepper. Serve separately.

Duck with Orange

4-pound duck
salt and pepper
½ ounce butter
2 large oranges
2 sugar lumps
1 tablespoon white wine
   vinegar
4 tablespoons dry white wine
1 tablespoon lemon juice

WIPE THE DUCK and season with salt and pepper. Dot with the butter and place in a roasting tin. Cook for 1 hour 20 minutes at Gas 6/400°F. Meanwhile, wash oranges and peel one. Cut the rind into strips like matchsticks, discarding the white bitter pith. Put the rind in a pan, cover with cold water and bring to the boil. Drain. Put sugar and vinegar in another pan with 1 tablespoon cold water. Heat for 10 minutes. Add the wine. Squeeze out and strain the juice of the peeled orange. Cut the remaining orange into thin slices. Add orange juice, rind and lemon juice to the sauce. Bring to the boil and boil for 5 minutes.

Arrange the cooked duck on a serving dish, garnish with the orange slices and pour on the sauce.
Serves 4

Roast Chicken

6-pound chicken
1 large lemon
4 ounces button mushrooms
  (chopped)
1 ounce streaky bacon
  (chopped)
4 ounces fresh white
  breadcrumbs
2 ounces butter
salt and pepper
ground nutmeg

WIPE THE CHICKEN and push the lemon into the body cavity. Mix the mushrooms and bacon and fry gently in a pan until soft. Stir in the breadcrumbs and 1 ounce butter until melted. Season with salt, pepper and nutmeg and mix with the egg. Use to stuff the neck end and plump out the breast.

Put the chicken in a roasting tin. Spread with the remaining butter and roast for $2\frac{1}{2}$ hours at 6/400°F.
Serves 6

1 large egg (beaten)

Roast Turkey

14–pound turkey
10 ounces fresh white
  breadcrumbs
3 ounces stoned raisins
3 ounces walnuts (chopped)
1 level tablespoon parsley
  (finely chopped)
2 ounces butter (melted)
salt and pepper
1 large egg (beaten)
2 pounds pork sausagemeat
2 level teaspoons mixed
  dried herbs
rind of 1 lemon (finely grated)
lard

WIPE TURKEY AND use giblets for stock for gravy (see page 114). Put 6 ounces breadcrumbs in a bowl with the raisins, walnuts, parsley and butter. Season with salt and pepper and mix with the egg. Use to stuff the neck end of the turkey and to plump out the breast. Mix the sausagemeat with the remaining crumbs, herbs and lemon rind. Season with salt and pepper. Use to stuff the body cavity. Stand the turkey in a roasting tin and spread with a little lard. Cook for about 6 hours at Gas 3/325°F. To test if done, push a skewer into the thickest part of the leg. No pink juices should run and you'll find the leg will move quite easily if cooked.
Serves 10

Bread Sauce

2 cloves
1 large onion (skinned)
1 small bay leaf
$\frac{1}{2}$ pint milk
2 ounces fresh white
  breadcrumbs
salt and pepper
cayenne pepper
1 ounce butter
2 tablespoons single cream

STICK THE CLOVES into the onion and place with the bay leaf in a small saucepan. Pour on the milk. Bring to the boil, then remove from the heat and leave to infuse for 30 minutes. Remove the onion and bay leaf and stir in the crumbs with salt, pepper and cayenne. Simmer gently for 5 minutes, then stir in the butter and cream, check seasoning and reheat gently.
Serves 6

Mince Pies

13-ounce packet frozen
   shortcrust pastry
12 ounces mincemeat
1 large egg (separated)
2 teaspoons cold water
2 ounces caster sugar
1 ounce unsalted butter
1 ounce icing sugar (sifted)
1 teaspoon lemon juice
   (strained)

ALLOW THE PASTRY to thaw at room temperature for at least 1 hour. Roll out on a lightly floured board and cut out 40 rounds using a 2-inch fluted cutter. Use 30 to line patty tins. Using a star cutter, cut stars from the centres of the remaining rounds. Fill the pastry cases with the mincemeat, moisten the edges of 10 cases and top them with star-shaped rounds and another 10 with the cut-out stars. Whisk the egg yolk with the water and use to brush these mince pies. Bake for about 20 minutes at Gas 6/400°F. Meanwhile, whisk the egg white until really stiff. Whisk in half the caster sugar, then gradually fold in the remainder keeping the meringue stiff. Top the open mince pies with this meringue and return to the oven for 5 minutes at Gas 8/450°F.

Cream the butter and icing sugar until light and fluffy. Gradually beat in the lemon juice. Spoon a little lemon butter cream into each of the star mince pies while still hot and serve at once.

Makes 30

Cumberland Rum Butter

8 ounces unsalted butter
1 pound soft brown sugar
4 tablespoons rum
ground nutmeg
ground cinnamon

BEAT THE BUTTER until soft and very pale. Gradually beat in the sugar, then beat in the rum a few drops at a time, making sure the mixture doesn't curdle. Add nutmeg and cinnamon to taste and spoon the mixture into small pots. Cover and store until required.

Brandy Butter

4 ounces unsalted butter
4 ounces caster sugar
3 tablespoons brandy

CREAM THE BUTTER until it is really pale, then beat in the sugar gradually. When well mixed beat in the brandy a few drops at a time. Take care the mixture does not curdle. Add the brandy slowly and beat the mixture vigorously between each addition. Pile into a glass dish and leave to harden.

Cheese Puff Fingers

8-ounce packet frozen puff
   pastry
3 ounces Cheddar cheese
   (grated)
1 ounce butter (creamed)

ALLOW THE PASTRY to thaw at room temperature for at least 1 hour. Mix the cheese into the butter and gradually beat in most of the egg. Season with salt and pepper and the mustard powder.

Roll the pastry on a lightly floured board to an oblong

1 large egg (beaten)
salt and pepper
¼ level teaspoon mustard
    powder
paprika

about 20 inches by 10 inches. Leave the pastry to rest for 10 minutes. Cut pastry in half and trim edges square. Spread the cheese mixture on one piece of pastry to within ½ inch of the edges. Moisten edges, cover with other piece of pastry and seal edges. Mark the pastry into fingers and carefully place on a damp baking sheet. Brush with the remaining egg.

Bake for about 15 minutes at Gas 6/400°F. Sprinkle with a little salt and paprika, allow to cool a little and then cut into fingers. Serve hot or warm.
Makes 20

Crown Roast

2 pieces best end neck of
    lamb (each with 7 or 8
    cutlets)
dripping
8-ounce packet frozen mixed
    vegetables
1 pound cooked potatoes
    (mashed)
1 ounce butter

ASK YOUR BUTCHER to prepare the two pieces of meat for a crown roast, scraping the ends of the bones clean. He will usually tie the two pieces of meat together but if not, turn them back to back and tie the two pieces to form the crown. Trim the meat and fat. Put the crown in a roasting tin, spread the meat with a little dripping and wrap a small piece of foil around each bone end to keep them white during cooking. Cook for 30 minutes per pound plus 30 minutes at Gas 4/350°F.

Five minutes before the roast is ready, cook the frozen vegetables. Beat the potato with the butter and keep hot. Arrange the crown roast on a serving plate and pipe mashed potato around the bottom. Fill the centre with the vegetables and top each bone with a cutlet frill. Serve with gravy and redcurrant jelly.
Serves 8

Mother's Day Cake

6 ounces butter
6 ounces caster sugar
3 large eggs (beaten)
6 ounces plain flour
pinch salt
2 level teaspoons baking
    powder
6 tablespoons lemon curd
glacé icing (see page 46)
2 or 3 empty egg shell halves
gold or silver paint
spring flowers
1-inch wide yellow ribbon

CREAM THE BUTTER with the sugar until light and fluffy. Gradually beat in the eggs, then fold in the flour, sifted with the salt and baking powder. Turn the mixture into 2 8-inch sandwich tins which should be greased and lined on the bases with greaseproof paper if not non-stick. Bake for about 25 minutes at Gas 4/350°F. Cool for 5 minutes in their tins, then turn on to wire racks.

When cold, spread one cake with lemon curd and sandwich with the other. Stand the cakes on a wire rack over a large dinner plate and coat with glacé icing to run all over the top and sides. Gather the drips from the plate and run glacé icing over the cake again once the first coat has set. Decorate with egg shell vases made as follows. Paint each egg shell half with gold or silver paint or with vegetable colourings. Fill with a little cotton wool moistened with water coloured dark green to colour the cotton wool and make it look like moss. Fill with spring flowers and arrange the shells in the centre of the cake, using a little icing to fix them in place if necessary. Tie a yellow ribbon round the cake and fasten with a bow.

Syllabub

¼ pint white wine
2 tablespoons brandy
1 large lemon
2 ounces caster sugar
½ pint double cream
ground cinnamon

POUR THE WINE and brandy into a small bowl. Thinly peel the rind from the lemon, removing all white pith from the peel. Squeeze out and strain the lemon juice. Put rind and juice with the brandy and leave for 24 hours. Next day, remove the lemon rind and stir in the sugar until it has dissolved. Add the cream and whip slowly until it begins to hold soft peaks. Sprinkle with a little cinnamon, whisk it in gently and turn the mixture into tiny delicate glasses. This mixture is very rich so it is quite all right to serve it in very small quantities. *Serves 8–10*

Simnel Cake

6 ounces butter
9 ounces caster sugar
3 large eggs (beaten)
8 ounces plain flour
1 level teaspoon baking powder
2 level teaspoons ground mixed spice
8 ounces sultanas
4 ounces currants
4 ounces seedless raisins
3 ounces glacé cherries (chopped)
3 ounces chopped mixed peel
milk to mix
6 ounces ground almonds
3 ounces icing sugar (sifted)
2 large egg yolks
Easter eggs
sugar mimosa
narrow gold ribbon

CREAM THE BUTTER with 6 ounces caster sugar until light and fluffy. Gradually beat in the eggs, then fold in the flour sifted with the baking powder and spice. Fold in the sultanas, currants, raisins, cherries, mixed peel and a little milk to make a stiff dropping consistency. Turn the mixture into an 8-inch round cake tin greased and lined with greaseproof paper. Hollow the centre of the mixture so it will have a flat top when baked. Bake for about 2 hours at Gas 3/325°F. Allow to cool in the tin, then remove on to a wire rack.

Mix the ground almonds with the remaining caster sugar and icing sugar and mix to a paste with the egg yolks. Roll almond paste to an 8-inch round and put on top of cake. Pinch the edge into a pattern between your thumb and forefinger. Decorate the top with small Easter eggs and sugar mimosa, if liked. Tie 2 bands of narrow gold ribbon round the cake.

Salted Nuts

½ pound walnut halves
½ pound whole almonds
2 ounces butter
2 tablespoons cooking oil
salt

USE ONLY WHOLE walnut halves and almonds. Heat 1 ounce butter with 1 tablespoon oil. Add the walnuts and fry for about 5 minutes, stirring all the time. Drain on kitchen paper while you fry the almonds in the remaining butter and oil. Drain and sprinkle all nuts with salt while still hot. Remove surplus salt for storage and keep in airtight tins.
Serves 8

Steak Diane

4 fillet steaks
1 small onion (chopped)
4 ounces butter
1 level tablespoon parsley
   (finely chopped)
Worcester sauce
1 dessertspoon lemon juice
   (strained)
salt and pepper
1 tablespoon brandy

FLATTEN EACH STEAK between two pieces of foil or waxed paper using your rolling pin. Each steak should be about ⅛-inch thick. Fry the onion in 1 ounce butter until transparent, but not browned. Remove the onion from the pan. Fry the steaks one after the other in the remaining butter (or in two frying-pans to speed the process) for about 1 minute on each side. Remove steaks and keep hot. Return the onion to one frying-pan. Stir in the parsley, Worcester sauce to taste, lemon juice and seasoning. Stir well, return the steaks to the pan. Pour on the brandy, heat well and light. Serve the steaks with the sauce poured over them.
Serves 4

Fondue Bourguignonne

horseradish sauce
tomato ketchup
chutney
tartare sauce
brown table sauce
1½ pounds rump steak
cooking oil

SPOON THE VARIOUS sauces into individual bowls and arrange on a small tray. Cut the meat into bite-sized pieces and arrange on individual plates. Heat the oil in a small pan or fondue pan and transfer to the table. Stand over a small spirit burner to keep it at the correct temperature throughout the cooking.

Spear a cube of meat and cook it in the hot oil. Dip it in the sauce of your choice and eat. Each person cooks his own steak as he likes it.
Serves 4

Red Cabbage with Apple

1 small red cabbage
3 rashers streaky bacon
1 ounce butter
1 small onion (chopped)
2 large cooking apples
  (chopped)
¼ pint boiling water
salt and pepper
3 dessertspoons Demerara
  sugar
3 tablespoons vinegar

REMOVE OUTER DAMAGED leaves from the cabbage and shred the remainder, discarding thick stalk and ribs. Put cabbage in a bowl of cold water. Cut off bacon rinds, chop rashers finely. Put rinds, bacon and butter in a saucepan and fry until bacon has browned and cooked. Remove rinds, add onion and cook gently for 5 minutes. Drain cabbage, add to pan, cover and fry gently for 5 minutes. Add apples, boiling water, salt and pepper to pan. Cover and simmer for about 1 hour until the water has been absorbed. Either uncover and cook till the water has been absorbed if there's any in the pan, or if the cabbage is really tender and won't stand any more cooking, pour away the excess. Stir in the sugar and vinegar. Cover and simmer for a further 5 minutes. Serve at once.
Serves 6

Cabbage Stuffed with Chestnuts

1 small firm cabbage
salt and pepper
10-ounce can whole chestnuts
1 ounce fresh white
  breadcrumbs
4 tablespoons milk
3 ounces butter
2 large onions (chopped)
4 ounces minced meat
  (cooked)
  (chicken, ham, beef or
  lamb)
2 pints chicken stock
2 carrots (sliced)
1 bay leaf
1 sprig thyme
parsley (finely chopped)

WASH THE CABBAGE and remove any outer damaged leaves, but keep the cabbage whole. Cook for about 15 minutes in plenty of boiling salted water. Drain well and separate the leaves, arranging them flat on a work surface. Cut out any thick ribs. Drain the chestnuts and reserve 3 whole ones for garnish. Mash the remainder. Soak the breadcrumbs in the milk. Melt the butter and cook the onions for about 10 minutes or until soft and just beginning to turn golden brown. Stir in the minced meat, mashed chestnuts and breadcrumbs which should be squeezed dry. Season well with salt and pepper. Spoon a little stuffing in the centre of each cabbage leaf and fold each one like a parcel to completely enclose the stuffing. Tie with cotton to keep in shape during cooking. Arrange the parcels in a pan, pour on the chicken stock and add the carrots, bay leaf and thyme. Bring to the boil, then simmer for 30 minutes. Drain and arrange on a serving dish, sprinkling them with the parsley and garnishing with the reserved chestnuts.
Serves 6

Sprouts in Cream

1 pound sprouts
salt and pepper
¼ pint double cream
1 level teaspoon ground
  coriander
1 teaspoon lemon juice
  (strained)

PREPARE THE SPROUTS and cook them in plenty of boiling salted water for about 20 minutes or until tender, but not soggy. Drain well and return to the pan with the cream, coriander, seasoning and lemon juice. Stir to heat the cream, then turn the sprouts into a dish.
Serves 4

Christmas Cake

8 ounces sultanas
10 ounces stoned raisins
1 pound currants
4 ounces chopped mixed peel
6 ounces glacé cherries
10 ounces plain flour
pinch salt
½ level teaspoon ground
  nutmeg
½ level teaspoon ground
  mixed spice
10 ounces butter
10 ounces Demerara sugar
rind of 1 lemon (finely
  grated)
6 large eggs (beaten)
2 tablespoons brandy
1 tablespoon lemon juice
  (strained)
almond paste (see page 107)
royal icing (see page 108)

MIX THE SULTANAS, raisins, currants, peel and cherries. Sift the flour, salt, nutmeg and mixed spice. Cream the butter and sugar until light and fluffy. Beat in the lemon rind and the eggs gradually, beating well after each addition. Add a little flour with the last of the egg. Fold in the flour and fruit mixtures alternately using a large spoon and mix to a stiff dropping consistency with the brandy and lemon juice. Turn the mixture into a greased and lined 9-inch round cake tin. Hollow the top so that it will bake to a flat surface. Bake for 4½ hours at Gas 2/300°F. covering the top when it seems to be brown enough. Leave to cool in the tin, then turn out on to a wire rack to complete the cooling. Leave on the papers and wrap the cake in foil and store in an airtight tin. If you don't have a large enough tin, the foil alone will suffice. Cover with almond icing at least two weeks before the cake is wanted and royal icing a week later.

Put a dab of icing in the centre of an 11-inch silver cake board and put the cake in the centre. Turn the icing on to the cake and using a palette knife, quickly cover the sides and top, swirling the icing or peaking it if preferred. If adding small decorations, it's worth noting that colourings sometimes run when put on wet icing. If icing is peaked, smooth small patches for the decorations otherwise they won't stand when the icing is dry. Smooth a place for the ribbon round the sides if liked. Leave to dry, then add decorations and ribbons and store in an airtight tin or well-wrapped in foil.

Christmas Pudding

10 ounces prunes
8 ounces stoned raisins
2 ounces plain flour
½ level teaspoon ground
  mixed spice
2 ounces Demerara sugar
2 ounces fresh white
  breadcrumbs
2 ounces currants
pinch salt
3 ounces shredded suet
1 large egg (beaten)
2 tablespoons brandy

SOAK PRUNES OVERNIGHT. Next day, drain and cover with fresh water. Boil for 15 minutes. Drain prunes, reserving 1 tablespoon of the liquid. Remove prune stones. Put all ingredients in a mixing bowl with re-served tablespoon of prune liquid. Mix well and turn into a 2-pint pudding basin. Cover loosely with foil and steam or boil for 4 hours. Steam or boil for another 2 hours before eating.
Serves 8

Roast Goose

10-pound goose
3 large onions (chopped)
2 ounces butter
1 heaped teaspoon dried sage
salt and pepper
8 ounces fresh white
  breadcrumbs

ASK YOUR BUTCHER to prepare the bird. Fry the onions in butter for 10 minutes or until really soft. Stir in the sage, salt and pepper and breadcrumbs. Stuff the rump end of the bird, pushing it into the body cavity. Secure with fine string or skewers. Prick the goose all over with a fork and stand the bird on a wire rack in the roasting tin. Cover it with butter papers. Cook for about 2½ hours at Gas 5/375°F. (or 15 minutes per pound plus 15 minutes extra if your goose is larger or smaller). Remove the butter papers during the last 30 minutes' cooking to allow the skin to crisp and become a good brown colour.

When the goose is cooked, lift it very carefully, for a lot of fat will run out of it. Serve on a large hot dish.
Serves 8

Cranberry Jelly

1 pound cooking apples
2 pounds cranberries
¼ pint fresh lemon juice
  (strained)
lump sugar

WASH AND CHOP the apples but don't peel them. Put cranberries, apples and lemon juice in a large pan. Just cover with cold water. Bring to the boil, then simmer for 40 minutes. Pour the pan of fruit through a jelly bag into another bowl or through several thicknesses of muslin. Don't squeeze the bag or try to hurry the process because the juice will be cloudy. When the juice has dripped through, measure it into a large clean pan. Add 1 pound sugar for every pint of juice. Heat gently, stirring all the time until the sugar has dissolved, then bring to the boil and boil to a set. Pour into clean hot jars and cover with waxed discs and transparent jampot covers. Store in a cool dark place and serve with roast turkey or with turkey pies.

Hot Cross Buns

½ ounce dried yeast
½ pint and 3 tablespoons
   tepid water
1 pound 5 ounces plain
   strong flour
½ level teaspoon salt
4 level teaspoons ground
   mixed spice
½ level teaspoon ground
   cinnamon
2 ounces lard
5 ounces granulated sugar
1 large egg (beaten)
3 ounces currants
1 ounce sultanas
½ ounce chopped mixed peel
4 tablespoons milk

SPRINKLE THE DRIED yeast on the warm water and leave it for 15 minutes or until frothy. Sift 1 pound 4 ounces flour, salt and spices and rub in the lard. Stir in 3 ounces sugar and make a well in the centre. Add the egg to the yeast mixture. Pour into the bowl and mix to a soft but not sticky dough. Knead the dough on a lightly floured surface. Put into an oiled bowl, cover with a wet cloth and leave in a warm place for 1 hour until double in size. Pull the dough from the sides of the bowl; it will be stringy if it's ready. Knead well again, kneading in the dried fruit and peel until evenly distributed. Divide into 18 equal pieces and shape each into a bun. Place 2 inches apart on greased baking sheets.

Mix the remaining flour with 2 tablespoons cold water to a thick paste and put it in a piping bag. Pipe a cross on each bun. Put in a warm place to prove for about 30 minutes. Bake for 15 minutes, or until risen and golden brown at Gas 7/425°F.

Heat rest of sugar and milk until the sugar has dissolved. Bring to boil and remove from heat. Remove cooked buns on to a wire rack and brush immediately with the sugar glaze. Leave to cool. Heat for 10 minutes before serving.

Recipe Index

General Index

barbecues, 8, 63–71
bonfire parties, 90
bonfire-night parties, 8, 113
buffet parties, 8, 14–28

cakes: christening, 98, 109; for children, 72; silver wedding, 98, 110; wedding, 97, 106
candles, use of, 9–10, 30, 63–4, 89
celebration parties, 97–110
centrepieces, 10, 29, 30, 99, 111
champagne, 99
children's parties, 8, 10, 81–8; see also toddlers' parties
christening cake, 98, 109
christening parties, 97
Christmas menus, 111
coats, where to put, 9
coffee: preparing, 30; recipes for, 39, 52, 101
coffee parties, 43–4
cutlery, see equipment, catering

desserts, quantities required per person, 16–17
dinner parties, 8, 29–42
displaying food, 14
doilies, 10, 73, 98, 99
drinks, 17, 30, 63, 83, 89, 99; for children, 72; quantities required per person, 17

Easter eggs, making and decorating, 112
economy entertaining, 30–1, 53–4
engagement parties, 9, 97
equipment, catering, 10, 13, 14, 63, 90

family parties, 8, 99
fish, quantities required per person, 16
flower arrangements, 29, 99
fruit, frosting, 10

games: for children, 81–2; for toddlers, 73
garden parties, 8; see also barbecues, bonfire parties, bonfire-night parties
garnishes, 54–5
gift for hostess, 13
glasses, see equipment, catering

Hallowe'en parties, 113
hostess: duties of a, 7; gift for, 13
hot cross buns, 112; recipe for, 123
hot-dog stall, 89–90

invitations, 8–9, 99

lighting, 9–10, 29, 63–4, 89, 113

meat, quantities required per person, 16
menu planning, 9, 15
mince pies, 111; recipe for, 116
Mother's Day, 112–13

napkins, 14, 63, 98; see also table-settings
napkin-folding, 10–12
New Year's Eve parties, 111–12
number of guests, deciding the, 8, 29

occasional parties, 111–23

pastries, quantities required per person, 16
planning, importance of, 7, 9, 15
plates, see equipment, catering
poultry, quantities required per person, 16
punch, 17

quantities of food, guide to, 15–17

sandwich fillings, quantities required per person, 15
silver wedding cake, 98; recipe for, 110
simnel cake, 112–13; recipe for, 118
supper parties, 53–62